Dhamma Now

Sarah Procter Abbott

2023

Published in 2023 by:
Zolag
www.zolag.co.uk

ISBN 9781897633472

Contents

Preface **vii**

1 August 2020 **1**

Zoom jottings 1 1

Conditions 1

Zoom jottings 2 2

The Best Medicine 2

Zoom jottings 3 4

Taking Refuge 4

Zoom jottings 4 5

The Examination 5

Zoom jottings 5 6

Āsavas 6

Zoom jottings 6 7

What is Vinaya? 7

Zoom jottings 7 9

The Truths 9

Zoom jottings 8 11

Understanding has to Develop 11

Zoom jottings 9 12

What is Practice? 12

Zoom jottings 10 13

The Meaning of Reality 13

Zoom jottings 11 16
Can Anyone Practice? 16
Zoom jottings 12 17
Can Anyone do Anything? 17
Zoom jottings 13 19
Is there any Short-cut? 19
Zoom jottings 14 20
Why Study Pāli? 20
Zoom jottings 15 22
4 Right Understandings and 4 Right Efforts . . . 22
Zoom jottings 16 24
What is there Now? 24
Zoom jottings 17 26
Enlightened to What? 26
Zoom jottings 18 27
Depending on Conditions 27

2 September 2020 **29**
Zoom jottings 19 29
Just do Your Best! 29
Zoom jottings 20 31
Virtue and Abandoning (Pahāna) 31
Zoom jottings 21 32
Once in Nowhere 32
Zoom jottings 22 33
The Empty World 33
Zoom jottings 23 35
Letting go of Desire for Understanding 35
Zoom jottings 24 36
Sammā Saṇkappa (Right Thinking) 36

3 October 2020 **39**
Zoom jottings 25 39
The World of Nimitta (Signs) 39
Zoom jottings 26 40
Burning 40
Zoom jottings 27 43
The Dear Self 43
Zoom jottings 28 44
Considering the True Words 44
Zoom jottings 29 45
The Proof of Understanding 45
Zoom jottings 30 46
Wrong Practice and Rituals 46
Zoom jottings 31 48
Study the Truth Respectfully 48
Zoom jottings 32 49
Soul 49
Zoom jottings 33 51
What is Now? 51
Zoom jottings 34 53
The Chief of Experiencing 53
Zoom jottings 35 54
Dhātu (Element) 54

4 November 2020 **57**
Zoom jottings 36 57
The Value of Patience 57
Zoom jottings 37 59
Anattā & Suññatā 59
Zoom jottings 38 60
Where is the World? 60
Zoom jottings 39 61
The Raft 61

Zoom jottings 40 63
The Magic Show 63
Zoom jottings 41 64
Why Bother? 64
Zoom jottings 42 66
The Bhikkhu's Life 66
Zoom jottings 43 67
Giving to a Bhikkhu or a Beggar 67
Zoom jottings 44 70
Hearing Again and Again 70
Zoom jottings 45 72
Preparation for Understanding 72
Zoom jottings 46 73
All Gone! 73
Zoom jottings 47 75
Once in Saṃsāra! 75

5 December 2020 77
Zoom jottings 48 77
Nutriment (Āhāra) 77

6 January 2021 81
Zoom jottings 49 81
Sīla (1) 81

7 February 2021 85
Zoom jottings 50 85
Sīla (2) 85
Zoom jottings 51 87
Ānāpānasati 87
Zoom jottings 52 88
Kusala (wholesome) or Akusala (unwholesome)
Cittas now? 88

8 March 2021 **91**
Zoom jottings 53 91
Ummagga, the “popping up” of Paññā 91
Zoom jottings 54 94
Bhava (existing) and Bhāva (nature) 94
Zoom jottings 55 95
Groups of Rūpas 95

9 April 2021 **99**
Zoom jottings 56 99
Sacca Pāramī (the perfection of truthfulness) . . 99
Zoom jottings 57 100
Meditation 100
Zoom jottings 58 102
Dreaming about how “I can do!” 102
Zoom jottings 59 103
Seeing in the Dark 103
Zoom jottings 60 104
Loss of a Dear Sister 104
Zoom jottings 61 107
Ordaining 107
Zoom jottings 62 110
The Worldly Conditions 110
Zoom jottings 63 111
Surgery 111
Biography 114
Further Study 114

Preface

When our trips to Vietnam, Taiwan and Thailand to study and share the Dhamma were cancelled due to Covid-19, Jonothan and I were delighted to assist Ajahn Sujin in offering Zoom discussions which have been very beneficial to many people around the world.

The "Jottings" I have made are based on these Zoom discussions.

Our discussions are always about the understanding of what is real, what is Dhamma now, as taught by the Buddha. Without careful consideration of this truth, as opposed to our usual assumptions of the way things are, there will never be an end to ignorance in life.

I have added a quote from the Buddhist scriptures to each "jotting" to show how these discussions relate to the original teachings of the Buddha.

With my great appreciation for the invaluable guidance given by Ajahn Sujin Boriharnwanaket over many decades, I offer this book to assist readers with the development of understanding in daily life.

I also wish to acknowledge the support of the publisher, Alan Weller, who encouraged me to publish these Zoom Jottings.

Sarah Procter Abbott

1

August 2020

Zoom jottings 1

Conditions

A friend, Jeff, had made a comment about giving more to people we meet.

Ajahn Sujin stressed that giving or not giving is by conditions, no matter what, not by anyone's control.

Understanding this is the only way that there will be less clinging, less attachment. If we try to change what is experienced the idea of "I" is there again.

Don't regret! Don't think about the past or future!

All conditioned dhammas are gone instantly or have not yet come!

> "Let not a person revive the past
> Or on the future build his hopes;
> For the past has been left behind
> And the future has not been reached.
> Instead with insight let him see
> Each presently arisen state."

> *Majjhima Nikāya 131 A Single Excellent Night (Translated by Bhikkhu Ñāṇamoli & Bhikkhu Bodhi)*

Zoom jottings 2

The Best Medicine

I had minor surgery yesterday and now the day at the hospital seems like a dream. It's all gone. Apparently during the surgery I was in some pain and asked the doctor to stop the operation at one point but afterwards I had no recollection of it. It's just like a nightmare which is forgotten when one wakes up or like experiences in former lives which we don't remember at all.

In one of the sessions Ajahn was referring to how good or bad situations don't belong to us. Whatever fortune or misfortune, happiness or unhappiness arises, it's just there for a moment. The world is just for a moment now and then gone completely.

When there is more understanding of the momentariness of dhammas (realities) in life as anattā (not self) there is freedom from the bondage of taking these worldly conditions (happiness and unhappiness, fame and insignificance, praise and blame, gain and loss) for something significant.

All day there is the taking of what is impermanent for permanent, what is not self for self, what is foul for beautiful and what is unsatisfactory for satisfactory. These are the perversions of thinking, memory and views, the vipallāsas as we read in the Vipallāsa Sutta:

> "Perceiving permanence in the impermanent, perceiving pleasure in what is suffering, perceiving a self in what is non-self, and perceiving attractiveness in what is unattractive, beings resort to wrong views, their minds deranged, their perception twisted.
>
> Such people are bound by the yoke of Mara, and do not reach security from bondage. Beings continue in saṃsāra, going to birth and death.
>
> But when the Buddhas arise in the world, sending forth a brilliant light, they reveal this Dhamma that leads to the stilling of suffering.
>
> Having heard it, wise people have regained their sanity. They have seen the impermanent as impermanent and what is suffering as suffering.
>
> They have seen what is non-self as non-self and the unattractive as unattractive. By the acquisition of right view, they have overcome all suffering."

Aṅguttara Nikāya 4:49 (9) Inversions (Translated by Bhikkhu Bodhi)

In reality there is no hospital, no surgery, no good or bad situation. There are just dhammas arising by their particular conditions and falling away instantly.

Understanding the truth as taught by the Buddha about the present moment is really the best medicine at any time.

Zoom jottings 3

Taking Refuge

Taking refuge means understanding the words of the Buddha, understanding that there is no self. No one can condition right understanding. A moment of understanding is taking refuge. The more understanding of the meaning of his words, the greater the refuge.

The refuge has to always be now. Don't mind which reality is experienced. Whatever arises is gone instantly. There can only ever be the understanding of what is experienced at this very moment.

A Vietnamese friend asked a question about the rule of behaviour for monks with regard to walking with eyes downcast. Like other rules to be followed, this can either be with attachment or with understanding of the right path. Just following conventional ideas about walking with downcast eyes with attachment doesn't lead to any understanding. The same applies to other rules if there is just the following of them without understanding the purpose of the Teachings. The purpose is always for the development of awareness and understanding of what appears now.

We read in the Visuddhimagga about "guarding" with awareness:

> "What is (proper) resort as guarding? Here 'A bhikkhu, having entered inside a house, having gone into a street, goes with downcast eyes, seeing the length of a plough yoke, restrained, not looking at an elephant, not looking at a horse, a carriage, a pedestrian, a woman, a man, not looking up, not looking down, not staring this way and that' (Nidd I 474). This is

> called (proper) resort as guarding."
>
> *Visuddhimagga 1 50 (Translated by Bhikkhu Ñāṇamoli)*

When there is "guarding", sati (awareness) and understanding arise and at such moments there is no attachment to what is seen. Naturally there will be less paying attention to the details. Usually we think a lot about what is seen and build up many stories about people and things, forgetting that it is only visible object which is seen and only seeing consciousness which sees for an instant and then they are gone forever. In truth there are no elephants or horses and no people at all no matter where we look.

Zoom jottings 4

The Examination

Ajahn Sujin stressed that whatever part of the Tipiṭaka it is, each word points to this moment.

Paññā (right understanding) knows what is meant by developing understanding. When a dhamma (reality) appears, nothing else appears. It knows that which experiences and that which is experienced.

Whatever arises does so by conditions. It seems normal and obvious, but the truth is very subtle.

We may be afraid of danger but whether there is danger or not, whatever the circumstances of life, there must be seeing, hearing and so on. In the deepest sense, each conditioned reality is dangerous because it arises and falls away and can be the object of clinging:

> "Friend Koṭṭhita, a virtuous bhikkhu should carefully attend to the five aggregates subject to clinging

> as impermanent, as suffering, as a disease, as a tumour, as a dart, as misery, as an affliction, as alien, as disintegrating, as empty, as non-self."
>
> *Saṃyutta Nikāya 22:122 (10) Virtuous (Translated by Bhikkhu Bodhi)*

Daily life is the examination. The Dhamma is not in the book! There has to be the understanding of the realities in daily life as "not me" or "mine". There has to be the understanding of the characteristic of what appears now instead of thinking about how much or how little understanding has been developed. Whatever appears and is known is according to the accumulation of understanding with no expectation of what will come next.

A friend had a birthday. The birthday is each day, each moment!

Zoom jottings 5

Āsavas

There was a discussion about how in truth there is no "me" and how there are just the realities in life, those which can experience and those which can only be experienced.

Lukas: I'm not interested in dhamma.
Ajahn Sujin: Always "I".

The second ariya sacca (Noble Truth) is lobha (attachment).

Ajahn Sujin continued to talk about the 4 āsavas, (the subtle taints or defilements which ooze out instantly after seeing, hearing and so on). Three of these are kinds of lobha, the clinging to sense objects (kāmāsava), the clinging to becoming (bhavāsava) and the clinging with wrong view (diṭṭhāsava). The other one is ignorance (avijjāsava).

Āsava refers to that which "flows out" like pus which oozes from an abscess or intoxicants which have been fermented for a long time. The taints are called āsavas because they are similar to pus oozing out and to fermented intoxicants.

> The āsavas are exuding: "from unguarded sense-doors like water from cracks in a pot, in the sense of constant trickling".
>
> *Visuddhimagga XXII 56 (Translated by Bhikkhu Ñāṇamoli)*

The light of understanding refers to what can be understood at this moment as not self. When it begins to develop and there is no desire or attachment as usual, it doesn't forget this moment. It understands that whatever arises is anattā, not in anyone's control.

When there is wanting all the time, like "wanting to come back to study or have good qualities", it leads to the wrong way. It is not understanding dhammas as not self and there is attachment to the cycle of birth and death all the time.

Now, the exam is at this moment of seeing and hearing, each reality arising and falling one at a time. Life goes on by conditions.

Zoom jottings 6

What is Vinaya?

A Vietnamese friend asked a question about the Vinaya and the following of rules. He said he had had discussions on this topic and he gave details about various situations and the conduct of the monks. He asked how to have more wise reflections when studying the Vinaya. He also mentioned some people find it a boring topic too.

All the rules are for the purpose of the development of satipaṭṭhāna, the development of awareness with right understanding of the Path. When paññā (right understanding) arises it knows what is meant by developing understanding of what appears. At such moments nothing else appears but the reality which is the world, the reality which experiences an object (nāma) or the reality which cannot experience anything (rūpa). Whatever part of the Tipiṭaka we read, it points to this moment, not to situations.

> "I say, friend, that by travelling one cannot know, see, or reach that end of the world where one is not born, does not grow old and die, does not pass away and get reborn. Yet I say that without having reached the end of the world there is no making an end of suffering. It is in this fathom-long body endowed with perception and mind that I proclaim (1) the world, (2) the origin of the world, (3) the cessation of the world, and (4) the way leading to the cessation of the world.
>
> The end of the world can never be reached by means of travelling [across the world]; yet without reaching the world's end there is no release from suffering.
>
> Hence the wise one, the world-knower,
> who has reached the world's end and lived the spiritual life,
> having known the world's end, at peace,
> does not desire this world or another."

Aṅguttara Nikāya 4:45 (5) Rohitassa 1 (Translated by Bhikkhu Bodhi)

What is Vinaya? "Vineti" (the verb in Pāli) means it leads away from akusala (unwholesome states). It leads out of saṃsāra (the cycle of life) through the removal of defilements. So the Vinaya refers to the understanding which leads out of saṃsāra.

Zoom jottings 7

The Truths

Nina raised the subject or wrong view. Ajahn stressed that it has to be understood as a reality. If it's not the object of understanding when it appears, it's only thinking about it.

A dhamma (reality) is not in Holland, not in Thailand, not in any place at all. It's just a reality. It's the wrong view that takes it as a self or thing or place. Only paññā (right understanding) can eradicate the idea of self as something permanent. Paññā is not self either. Whatever arises is a dhamma (reality), not self.

Sacca ñāṇa is the firm intellectual understanding of the Four Noble Truths beginning with the 1st Noble Truth of Dukkha (unsatisfactoriness). Dukkha is that reality which arises and falls away. The 2nd, 3rd and 4th Noble Truths can not be known if the 1st Truth is not understood. What is the truth at this moment? This moment is the 1st Truth, dukkha. The 2nd Truth is that lobha (attachment) is the cause of dukkha. It is more difficult to understand the truth of it. Any truth, any reality appearing, is to be known now otherwise there will never be even the understanding of the 1st Truth.

As we read in the 1st sermon spoken by the Buddha in the Dhammacakkappavattana Sutta:

> "This noble truth of suffering is to be fully understood."
> "This noble truth of the origin of suffering is to be abandoned."
> "This noble truth of the cessation of suffering is to be realized."
> "This noble truth of the way leading to the cessation of suffering is to be developed."
>
> *Saṃyutta Nikāya 56:11 Setting in Motion the Wheel of the Dhamma (Translated by Bhikkhu Bodhi)*

> "The truth of suffering is to be compared with a disease, the truth of the origin of suffering with the cause of the disease, the truth of extinction of suffering with the cure of the disease, the truth of the path with the medicine."
>
> *Visuddhimagga XVI 87 (Translated by Bhikkhu Ñāṇamoli)*

What is the purpose of listening? Each word brings about the understanding as taught by the Buddha. Paññā understands the truth as the truth. Because of attachment there's no understanding of what arises and falls away. Instead there is attachment to what has already gone or not yet come almost all the time. This is why the 2nd truth doesn't appear yet. The 4 āsavas (taints or very subtle defilements) of kāmāsava (clinging to sense objects), bhavāsava (clinging to existing), avijjāsava (ignorance) and diṭṭhāsava (wrong view) arise after seeing and hearing all day long, quite unknown.

Zoom jottings 8

Understanding has to Develop

There has been further discussion about the āsavas (taints). These are kāmāsava (clinging to sense objects), bhavāsava (clinging to existing), avijjāsava (ignorance) and diṭṭhāsava (wrong view). The reason that the Buddha taught about these āsavas is to show how ignorance and attachment "ooze" out even in the sense door processes, long before there is any idea of anyone or anything. So even now as we read and study dhamma, there is no knowing at all about these very subtle defilements.

The understanding of anattā (not self) of all realities has to develop from intellectual right understanding to satipaṭṭhāna to vipassanā ñāṇa. Vipassanā ñāṇas refer to different levels of insight when the realities appear very clearly in succession. After the vipassanā ñāṇas the pariññās (understanding as realisations) apply what has been understood by the vipassanā ñāṇas, that which hasn't been understood clearly before. What has been realised clearly is "applied" to other objects of understanding.

In the beginning, when intellectual right understanding develops, the understanding of realities is not enough to condition direct understanding of what appears. Even when it is direct understanding, satipaṭṭhāna, the moments of understanding of dhammas as anattā are not sufficient and not clear enough to overcome doubts and wrong view.

Gradually, through the growth of right understanding there's more and more understanding that sati (awareness) is not "my awareness" and paññā (understanding) is not "my understanding. It depends on paññā to see what hinders the knowing of dhammas as realities. This hindrance is attachment and especially attachment with wrong understanding, clinging to the idea that "I can be aware" or "I can follow the path". The 2nd Noble

Truth of lobha (attachment) as the cause of dukkha and life in saṃsāra cannot be known in the beginning.

With regard to the 3rd Noble Truth, dukkha nirodha (the cessation of dukkha), if there is no understanding of the 1st Truth of dukkha, how can there be the understanding of the ending of all conditioned realities, the end of dukkha? If there is no understanding of the danger of what arises and falls away there cannot be the understanding of the 3rd Truth. For this understanding there must be the understanding of the arising and falling away of dhammas by conditions. If there are no conditions, nothing arises.

> "Of all those things that arise from a cause,
> The Tathagata has explained the cause;
> And how they cease to be has also been explained,
> This is the doctrine of the Great Recluse."
>
> "Yē dhammā hetuppabhavā
> tesam hetum Tathāgato āha,
> tesanca yo nirodho
> evam vādī Mahāsamano tī"
>
> *Peṭakopadesa 1 (Translated by Bhikkhu Nyanaponika)*

Zoom jottings 9

What is Practice?

Each word of the Buddha is precious. It's now!

A friend asked about practice in a Chinese discussion.

Ajahn Sujin: What does it mean?

Answer: A standardised procedure to get something, about doing something.

AS: What is doing and what is it for?

Answer: To have more wisdom.

AS: So it's "I want to get something". Is seeing "doing"? Is there anyone to do anything? When there's no understanding, what is doing?

I talked about bhāvanā, the development of understanding. It's not following a practice or anyone doing anything. It begins with understanding one word at a time. This is the beginning of understanding of paññā (right understanding) which conditions the development of all kusala (wholesome) states.

> "Bhikkhus, just as the dawn is the forerunner and precursor of the sunrise, so right view is the forerunner and precursor of wholesome qualities."
>
> *Aṅguttara Nikāya 10:121 (9) Forerunner (Translated by Bhikkhu Bodhi)*

The difference between ignorance and right understanding can be understood now. Pariyatti (intellectual right understanding) is learning to understand reality now. It must be the understanding of not self, firmer and firmer. So if someone says a self exists, this firm understanding knows it's not true.

From birth to death, there is nothing but the arising of realities, but it's unknown. If there is no understanding, there is just ignorance from birth to death for aeons and aeons, non-stop!

Zoom jottings 10

The Meaning of Reality

It's essential to know the purpose of listening and considering. If it's not for understanding of whatever appears now then it's bound to be for oneself. We discussed this topic in a Chinese session.

Ajahn Sujin: What appears now?

Answer: Reflecting on what you're saying, my foot on the floor, observing hardness.

AS: Different realities or just one? Is there wanting to observe, wanting to be aware? This is just a story about realities, not the nature of reality as anattā.

Sound is just that which appears. Understand a reality as it is, not my voice or the sound of music, just sound. Gradually this is the way to eliminate the idea of something or someone, no one there at all. For example, when the sound "nāma" is heard, there's no understanding yet, but it must be different from another sound, "rūpa". The idea of "I" is there all the time because what appears is not distinguished from other realities. At the moment the sound appears, it's not the same as the meaning of the word. It doesn't appear well because there's no understanding of the sound as just sound.

There has to be understanding of the meaning of dhamma (reality). Without understanding each dhamma as it is, it won't be known that there is nothing else at all. There has to be the understanding of how the story of sound is different from the moment when sound appears.

To be truthful, is there any understanding of sound yet? There is usually ignorance of sound that is heard, there is the idea of "my" sound or the sound of music. In truth it's just sound which falls away instantly.

Life is like this from moment to moment. Each reality has its characteristic by conditions and is uncontrollable, never to return again. This is the beginning of understanding life and the world and what is meant by "dhamma". No one is there, no one is in the room, there are just different realities. When there is no understanding there is the idea of something all the time, the idea of the sound of this and that.

> "Suppose, bhikkhus, there was a king or a royal minister who had never before heard the sound of a lute. He might hear the sound of a lute and say: 'Good man, what is making this sound—so tantalizing, so lovely, so intoxicating, so entrancing, so enthralling?' They would say to him: 'Sire, it is a lute that is making this sound—so tantalizing, so lovely, so intoxicating, so entrancing, so enthralling.' He would reply: 'Go, man, bring me that lute.'
>
> They would bring him the lute and tell him: 'Sire, this is that lute, the sound of which was so tantalizing, so lovely, so intoxicating, so entrancing, so enthralling.' The king would say: 'I've had enough with this lute, man. Bring me just that sound.' The men would reply: 'This lute, sire, consists of numerous components, of a great many components, and it gives off a sound when it is played upon with its numerous components; that is, in dependence on the parchment sounding board, the belly, the arm, the head, the strings, the plectrum, and the appropriate effort of the musician. So it is, sire, that this lute consisting of numerous components, of a great many components, gives off a sound when it is played upon with its numerous components.'
>
> The king would split the lute into ten or a hundred pieces, then he would reduce these to splinters. Having reduced them to splinters, he would burn them in a fire and reduce them to ashes, and he would winnow the ashes in a strong wind or let them be car-

> ried away by the swift current of a river. Then he would say: 'A poor thing, indeed sir, is this so-called lute, as well as anything else called a lute. How the multitude are utterly heedless about it, utterly taken in by it!' "
>
> *Saṃyutta Nikāya 35:246 (9) The Simile of the Lute (Translated by Bhikkhu Bodhi)*

In truth there never was, is or will be a lute. There is just sound that is heard and just thinking about all kinds of ideas about what is heard now.

Zoom jottings 11

Can Anyone Practice?

The discussion about practice and anattā continued in a Chinese discussion,

Ajahn Sujin stressed that to understand the meaning of reality as not self, there must be the understanding of each reality. Hearing, memory, feeling, like and dislike are all suññatā and anattā. Without proper conditions they cannot arise. This is why they are anattā, uncontrollable.

Sound is not my voice and seeing is not my seeing. We need to begin to consider the words of the Buddha respectfully because it's not easy to directly understand the truth of realities.

We use many words without understanding them, such as awareness. Seeing is seeing now, not a moment ago. Without listening and considering carefully there cannot be the clear understanding of what the Buddha taught.

What is nāma now at this moment of seeing? What about understanding now? It has to be one's own understanding, not the other's. Is it direct understanding now?

"I hear", "I think", is it right? When there's no clear understanding, it cannot eradicate the idea of self. Hearing about pariyatti (intellectual right understanding) is only the story of what arises.

Can anyone practice?

> "Bhikkhus, the eye is non-self. What is non-self should be seen as it really is with correct wisdom thus: 'This is not mine, this I am not, this is not my self.'
>
> The ear is non-self... The nose is non-self... The tongue is non-self... The body is non-self... The mind is non-self. What is non-self should be seen as it really is with correct wisdom thus: 'This is not mine, this I am not, this is not my self.'
>
> "Seeing thus... He understands: '... there is no more for this state of being.' "
>
> *Saṃyutta Nikāya 35:3 (3) The Internal as Non-self (Translated by Bhikkhu Bodhi)*

Zoom jottings 12

Can Anyone do Anything?

Ariya Kamma asked during a Chinese discussion whether we should stay in a good mood or "adjust kamma and cultivate kusala kamma". She asked how to avoid cittas which are "frustrated and inferior" and can condition disease. According to the book, one should avoid inferior states. If there is no practice, how is this possible?

Ajahn Sujin asked her if anyone can do anything or whether there are only realities. What is there now? Is there "I" now or just seeing which arises to see? Without citta, the body cannot move or do anything.

Is life "my life" or what is life now? Practice, what is it? What's the purpose of practising?

Ariya Kamma answered the purpose is to cultivate the habit to 'stay awake'. Someone else mentioned to 'manage akusala to kusala'.

What is the difference between practising and understanding? At the moment of understanding, it's clear that no one is practising. Right understanding has to be developed from moment to moment, but not by an imaginary Self. We talked further about bhāvanā (mental development), sati (awareness), paññā (understanding) and how they are not self. We also discussed awareness and awakening. When there is seeing, is there any awakening? When seeing arises, it arises with seven cetasikas (mental factors), no one can make more arise. When there's an idea of changing the reality now, it's not understanding anattā.

Only when there is firmer confidence can there be the understanding of different realities. Without careful study there's always the idea of "I want to understand". When there's more understanding about the cittas before and after seeing, gradually there's more understanding of no self. Who could make or determine what cittas arise in an eye-door process? Seeing is only a moment of experiencing no matter it's the ant's or the elephant's seeing. What is is seen is not a floor, a table or any thing at all. It's just the visible object which appears now.

> "Bhikkhus, form is non-self. For if, bhikkhus, form were self, this form would not lead to affliction, and it would be possible to have it of form: 'Let my form be thus; let my form not be thus.' But because

form is non-self, form leads to affliction, and it is not possible to have it of form: 'Let my form be thus; let my form not be thus.'

Feeling is non-self... Perception is non-self... Volitional formations are non-self... Consciousness is non-self. For if, bhikkhus, consciousness were self, this consciousness would not lead to affliction, and it would be possible to have it of consciousness: 'Let my consciousness be thus; let my consciousness not be thus.' But because consciousness is non-self, consciousness leads to affliction, and it is not possible to have it of consciousness: 'Let my consciousness be thus; let my consciousness not be thus.' "

Saṃyutta Nikāya 22:59 The Characteristic of Non-Self (Translated by Bhikkhu Bodhi)

Zoom jottings 13

Is there any Short-cut?

We had a discussion about the First Noble Truth (ariya sacca) in a Chinese session.

This is the truth about dhammas (realities). Whatever arises is conditioned. It's dukkha (unsatisfactory). Is dukkha known to paññā? Is it the absolute truth now or just an idea? Ignorance cannot tell.

Paṭipatti doesn't mean practice at all. If there is no clear understanding of reality now, one at a time, it's impossible to understand the arising and falling away of a reality. Paṭipatti is that which reaches the particular object to be known, the direct understanding.

Ariya Kamma asked about the objects of samatha bhāvana.

Ajahn Sujin: Can samatha bhāvana understand reality now?
AK: Yes.
AS: As self.
AK: As a short-cut.
AS: Then there must have been Sammā Sambuddha before the Buddha's Teachings!

> " 'What do you think, bhikkhu, is the eye permanent or impermanent?'–'Impermanent, venerable sir'. . . 'Is the ear . . . the nose . . . the tongue . . . the body . . . the mind . . . mind-consciousness . . . mind-contact . . . whatever feeling arises with mind-contact as condition–whether pleasant or painful or neither-painful-nor-pleasant, permanent or impermanent?' – 'Impermanent, venerable sir.'–'Is what is impermanent suffering or happiness?'–'Suffering, venerable sir.'–'Is what is impermanent, suffering, and subject to change fit to be regarded thus: "This is mine, this I am, this is my self?"'–'No, venerable sir.' "
>
> *Saṃyutta Nikāya 35:75 (2) Sick (Translated by Bhikkhu Bodhi)*

Zoom jottings 14

Why Study Pāli?

Maeve asked a question about the development of the Path and accumulations in an English discussion.

Ajahn Sujin explained that the development of paññā (right understanding) understands accumulations now from moment to moment. There are always conditions for ignorance and akusala (unwholesome states) such as attachment now, but not always conditions for paññā. When there is more paññā, there are more pāramī (perfections) to understand the truth.

Maeve asked another question about the use of Pāli terms and language.

AS: What's the purpose of studying in Pāli? Can you understand Pāli better than your own language? Even in the Buddha's time could the person who spoke Pāli understand seeing consciousness? Any word which can bring about understanding of reality now is the right word. For example, seeing or cakkhu viññāna - which conditions more understanding?

As understanding grows it understands more about the depth of ignorance and attachment. Even though we are talking about dhamma, there is not understanding of the depth of dhamma. For example, we're talking about seeing but does it appear now?

Is attachment understood now?

> "Puṇṇa, there are forms cognizable by the eye that are desirable, lovely, agreeable, pleasing, sensually enticing, tantalizing. If a bhikkhu seeks delight in them, welcomes them, and remains holding to them, delight arises in him. With the arising of delight, Puṇṇa, there is the arising of suffering, I say. There are, Puṇṇa, sounds cognizable by the ear... mental phenomena cognizable by the mind that are desirable, lovely, agreeable, pleasing, sensually enticing, tantalizing. If a bhikkhu seeks delight in them, welcomes them, and remains holding to them, delight arises in him. With the arising of delight, Puṇṇa, there is the arising of suffering, I say."

Saṃyutta Nikāya 35:88 (5) Puṇṇa (Translated by Bhikkhu Bodhi)

Zoom jottings 15

4 Right Understandings and 4 Right Efforts

In a Vietnamese discussion there was mention of the 4 sampajaññas (understandings) and also the 4 padhānas (right efforts).

Sampajañña is paññā (understanding). Sati-sampajañña refers to awareness and understanding, as referred to in the development of satipaṭṭhāna.

In brief these are:

a) **sātakkha sampajañña** - sātakkha means what is the purpose or what is beneficial. The understanding of what is beneficial or good from knowing what is the purpose of the right understanding of realities.

b) **sappāya sampajañña** - sappāya means what is suitable. Understanding what is suitable for the path.

c) **gocara sampajañña** - gocara means object (ārammaṇa) or field of experience. Here it refers to the object for right understanding, such as visible object which appears now.

d) **asammoha sampajañña** - asammoha is the opposite of ignorance. It refers to understanding of reality now without ignorance.

There was a question about the 4 right efforts (sammā padhāna) which are sammā vāyāma of the 8 fold Path.

1. the effort to avoid (saṃvara-padhāna)

2. the effort to overcome (pahāna-padhāna)
3. the effort to develop (bhāvanā-padhāna)
4. the effort to maintain (anurakkhaṇa-padhāna)

No self is involved from beginning to end. Viriya cetasika arises by conditions and when it arises with right understanding it is right effort.

Saṃvara-padhāna refers to the effort to avoid unwholesome states. Now at moments of wise consideration, there is such restraining from what is unprofitable or unwholesome states not yet arisen.

Pahāna-padhāna refers to the effort overcome unwholesome states. At moments of understanding, there is abandoning of unwholesome states that have arisen.

Bhāvanā-padhāna refers to the effort to develop wholesome states not yet arisen. At moments of understanding with right effort, there is the arising of profitable states not yet arisen.

Anurakkhaṇa-padhāna refers to the effort to maintain the wholesome states. The profitable states that have arisen are maintained and developed.

> "Bhikkhus, there are these four right strivings. What four? (1) Here, a bhikkhu generates desire for the non-arising of unarisen bad unwholesome states; he makes an effort, arouses energy, applies his mind, and strives. (2) He generates desire for the abandoning of arisen bad unwholesome states; he makes an effort, arouses energy, applies his mind, and strives. (3) He generates desire for the arising of unarisen wholesome states; he makes an effort, arouses energy, applies his mind, and strives. (4) He generates desire for the persistence of arisen wholesome states,

> for their non-decline, increase, expansion, and fulfilment by development; he makes an effort, arouses energy, applies his mind, and strives. These are the four right strivings."
>
> *Aṅguttara Nikāya 4:13 (3) Striving (Translated by Bhikkhu Bodhi)*

It may seem that such terms are in the book, but they are referring to the realities now which are conditioned at moments of right understanding.

Zoom jottings 16

What is there Now?

Ngoc Dang asked a question in a Vietnamese discussion about pariyatti, reading, listening, hearing and practice, paṭipatti. Should we notice or practice?

It was pointed out that pariyatti (intellectual right) understanding from reading, listening and considering what is true begins with very little right consideration and understanding to more and more understanding. From the beginning it's not "me" or "you" who understands, but understanding arising by conditions. It leads to paṭipatti (direct) understanding and eventually to paṭivedha understanding or direct realisation, vipassanā ñāṇa up to enlightenment.

No matter what level of understanding it is, it must be the understanding of what appears now. This may be sound or hearing or thinking of whatever reality appears now. Usually because of ignorance it's taken for some thing or some one all the time.

Pariyatti is not just a word that we're interested to talk about, it's understanding now! Without the Teachings we don't know what is what. We just want to understand the word but don't know what it's about. When we hear the words, there can be the beginning of understanding what is there now. From not knowing anything, there is the beginning of understanding of what appears at this moment.

Another listener mentioned that inside she feels very nervous and always thinks about "I" or "you" or "he" or "she". Also, when there is anger, she tries to be aware and follow the words of the Buddha.

Ajahn Sujin: Forget about trying to follow the words of the Buddha. Just consider what the truth is now. There are moments of anger, seeing, thinking and so on. Can it be "I" or someone or some thing?

The way to develop understanding is to understand at this moment. What is there now? What is real now? There's no way to do anything.

Someone else asked how she can accumulate paññā?

AS: Does paññā want anything? Wanting, wishing, craving all the time. Each word should be understood as letting go! Letting go of what? Let go of craving. Whenever there is the idea of "how can I", it indicates no understanding of dhamma.

Hearing and considering leads to firmer confidence. No one can make it happen. Without khanti (patience), sacca (truthfulness), adiṭṭhāna (determination) and viriya (effort) pāramī, it's impossible to understand reality now.

Zoom jottings 17

Enlightened to What?

Thao asked about meditation and the Buddha's enlightenment in a Vietnamese discussion. He asked about samatha and the intention to sit still to calm the mind.

Ajahn Sujin: Who is meditating? Can anyone meditate? Can anyone calm the mind?

T: I can do that. I will set the mind. I can clear the mind. When the Buddha understood the truth, he was sitting under the tree meditating. There is clarity of mind from sitting, relaxing.

AS: Let's consider one word at a time. He was enlightened to what? He understood the truth of what? He was enlightened to the truth of seeing, hearing, everything. So what did he say about seeing which he had been enlightened to? Is the mind dirty or clean? Some people try to make it clear or clean by some method, but it's so very dirty with ignorance.

There was a discussion about pariyatti leading to the direct understanding, satipaṭṭhāna. Bhāvanā is the development of understanding. Vipassanā is the clear understanding of realities as they are. Right understanding has to be very firm to condition the direct understanding of a reality now.

Hearing and wise considering leads to the end of ignorance and the end of all kilesa (defilements). Before hearing the Teachings, everything is "me", "I", but after hearing the Teachings that there are just realities which are gone, never to return. There is the development of the understanding of the Truth, but not yet the direct understanding. Just listen!

> "Bhikkhus, without directly knowing and fully understanding the all, without developing dispassion

towards it and abandoning it, one is incapable of destroying suffering.

And what, bhikkhus, is the all...?

The eye and forms and eye-consciousness and things to be cognized by eye-consciousness. The ear and sounds and ear-consciousness and things to be cognized by ear-consciousness... The mind and mental phenomena and mind-consciousness and things to be cognized by mind-consciousness.

This, bhikkhus, is the all without directly knowing and fully understanding which, without developing dispassion towards which and abandoning which, one is incapable of destroying suffering.

But, bhikkhus, by directly knowing and fully understanding the all, by developing dispassion towards it and abandoning it, one is capable of destroying suffering."

Saṃyutta Nikāya 35:27 Full Understanding (2) (Translated by Bhikkhu Bodhi)

Zoom jottings 18

Depending on Conditions

Whatever arises depends on paccaya, conditions. We discussed this topic further in a Vietnamese session. Without the understanding of the various dhammas as being conditioned, there can never be the second stage of insight, the paccaya pariggaha ñāṇa, (the clear understanding of the conditioned nature of dhammas). There is no one at all, just kusala, akusala, vipāka (result), kiriya (inoperative) cittas and rūpas arising by various conditions.

Each word of the Buddha will lead to the understanding of what appears now, little by little. There should be no selection or expectation of what will arise, no choosing at all. The future hasn't come and the past has gone. The Buddha didn't say "Do that"! It's impossible. When it's taught by anyone to do or to try to do anything, it's not the word of the Enlightened One.

The Teachings are so subtle and profound. If this were not so, there would not be the vipassanā ñāṇas, the clear insights of different degrees of paṭivedha understanding.

Right understanding is the "forerunner" like the dawn. Without right understanding there can never be any development of the Path.

> "Bhikkhus, this is the forerunner and precursor of the rising of the sun, that is, the dawn. So too, bhikkhus, for a bhikkhu this is the forerunner and precursor of the breakthrough to the Four Noble Truths as the really are, that is, right view. It is to be expected that a bhikkhu with right view will understand as it really is: 'This is suffering'... 'This is the way leading to the cessation of suffering.' "

Saṃyutta Nikāya 56:37 (7) The Sun (1) (Translated by Bhikkhu Bodhi)

2

September 2020

Zoom jottings 19

Just do Your Best!

In an English discussion, a friend mentioned her mother was dying in hospital and she was dependent on a breathing tube. Her mother wants her children to remove it. She wonders whether this is killing.

Ajahn Sujin reminded her that when someone dies it depends on kamma. The tube may be removed but she may continue to live or may die before it's removed. It depends on one's intention. One just does the best for one's mother at the time.

Everyone is going to die, but we don't know when. The

death moment can arise anytime, even now! The best thing is to understand realities as not self, no one at all, to gradually eliminate the idea of self. When there's the idea of I, I know a lot, I know a little, there's no way to understand reality now. However, when there's understanding of reality now, death or anything can be understood as dhamma. The right intellectual understanding develops on and on to be the condition for direct understanding, not just to understand words. It's the only way to understand that each word represents reality as not self.

Jeff also mentioned world conflicts and we discussed about the worlds at each moment, through the 6 doorways. Whatever arises and falls away now is a world.

> "Then a certain bhikkhu approached the Blessed One... and said to him: "Venerable sir, it is said, 'the world, the world.' In what way, venerable sir, is it said 'the world'?"
>
> 'It is disintegrating, bhikkhu, therefore it is called the world. And what is disintegrating? The eye, bhikkhu, is disintegrating, forms are disintegrating, eye-consciousness is disintegrating, eye-contact is disintegrating, and whatever feeling arises with eye-contact as condition... that too is disintegrating. The ear is disintegrating... The mind is disintegrating... Whatever feeling arises with mind-contact as condition...-that too is disintegrating. It is disintegrating, bhikkhu, therefore it is called the world.' "
>
> *Saṃyutta Nikāya 35:82 The World (Translated by Bhikkhu Bodhi)*

Zoom jottings 20

Virtue and Abandoning (Pahāna)

A friend asked us in a Vietnamese discussion about virtue, abandoning (pahāna) and non-transgression. I referred to some of the different kinds of abandoning (pahāna) as given in the texts. These are:

1. Tadaṅga pahāna refers to the partial elimination of self view and vitikammma kilesa (strong defilements) through the vipassanā ñāṇas (insights). Ordinary kusala can be tadaṅga (temporary elimination of akusala), but it's not pahāna unless it is vipassanā ñāṇa which begins to abandon kilesa. Each vipassana ñāṇa is therefore tadaṅga pahāna.

2. Vikkambhana pahāna refers to different levels of samādhi, specifically to jhāna which temporarily suppresses and overcomes pariyuṭṭhāna (subtle) kilesa.

3. Samuccheda pahāna refers to the function of the four magga cittas to eradicate anusaya (latent tendency) kilesa at various stages when realizing Nibbāna. Samuccheda is the "cutting off".

4. Paṭippassaddhi pahāna refers to the path knowledge when any of the four magga cittas arise. The knowledge of Nibbāna is realized.

5. Nissaraṇa pahāna refers to Nibbāna itself.

Now when there is any understanding of realities, it is the beginning of the path leading to abandoning of defilements, the beginning of "abandoning" of kilesa (defilements).

> "And what are the things to be abandoned neither by body nor by speech but by having repeatedly seen with wisdom? Greed is to be abandoned neither by body nor by speech but by having repeatedly seen with wisdom. Hatred... Delusion... Anger... Hostility ... Denigration... Insolence... Miserliness is to be abandoned neither by body nor by speech but by having repeatedly seen with wisdom."
>
> *Aṅguttara Nikāya, 10:23 (3) Body (Translated by Bhikkhu Bodhi)*

Zoom jottings 21

Once in Nowhere

"Where are we?" Ajahn Sujin asked everyone in a Vietnamese discussion. Nowhere at all! Where is seeing, just seeing? It's only the idea of somewhere. This is the way to understand about nothing, nowhere at all. Once in nowhere! Apart from the absolute truth, there is nothing else. If one thinks otherwise, there's always the idea of I am sitting somewhere, not understanding that each reality has gone completely.

The best thing is to understand what is at this moment, no "I" at all, nothing. Only such understanding can lead to the end of saṃsāra (the cycle of births and deaths). When there is no precise understanding, there cannot be the idea of no self. There has to be understanding which develops gradually. Is there the beginning of understanding at this moment? Otherwise there is always the idea of I know, I understand, I learn and I listen, when actually there is no "I" at all from the very beginning.

So where are you now? Each reality arises once in saṃsāra only.

There was a question about going forth and the meaning of nekkhamma (renunciation). No matter where you are, whenever there is no understanding there is no getting away from or renunciation of the wrong idea of self. The clinging is to sense objects and whatever is taken for self. Now if right understanding arises, it is moving away from wrong understanding little by little. It's not easy at all to take away clinging to the idea of self and things.

> "There are, Migajāla, sounds cognizable by the ear... odours cognizable by the nose... tastes cognizable by the tongue... tactile objects cognizable by the body... mental phenomena cognizable by the mind that are desirable, lovely, agreeable, pleasing, sensually enticing, tantalizing. If a bhikkhu seeks delight in them... he is called one dwelling with a partner.
>
> Migajala, even though a bhikkhu who dwells thus resorts to forests and groves, to remote lodgings where there are few sounds and little noise, desolate, hidden from people, appropriate for seclusion, he is still called one dwelling with a partner. For what reason? Because craving is his partner, and he has not abandoned it; therefore he is called one dwelling with a partner."
>
> *Saṃyutta Nikāya 35:61 Migajāla (1) (Translated by Bhikkhu Bodhi)*

Zoom jottings 22

The Empty World

In the Vietnamese discussion, we discussed how we think we're living in the world but we're not there because there are only conditioned realities arising and falling away. Only paññā can understand the difference between the imaginary world and the world of realities arising and falling away. When reality appears, there is nothing, no person at all. Without understanding there is always something or someone.

In fact the world is empty, empty of anything or anyone.

> "Then the Venerable Ānanda approached the Blessed One... and said to him: Venerable sir, it is said, 'Empty is the world, empty is the world.' In what way, venerable sir, is it said, 'Empty is the world'?
>
> 'It is, Ānanda, because it is empty of self and of what belongs to self that it is said, 'Empty is the world.' And what is empty of self and of what belongs to self? The eye, Ānanda, is empty of self and of what belongs to self. Forms are empty of self and of what belongs to self. Eye-consciousness is empty of self and of what belongs to self. Eye-contact is empty of self and of what belongs to self... Whatever feeling arises with mind-contact as condition—whether pleasant or painful or neither-painful-nor-pleasant--that too is empty of self and of what belongs to self.
>
> It is, Ānanda, because it is empty of self and of what belongs to self that it is said, 'Empty is the world.' "

Saṃyutta Nikāya 35:85 (2) (Translated by Bhikkhu Bodhi)

There is nothing to do at all, just listen to the right words of the Buddha until there is confidence in what appears now as it is. The flux of the arising and falling away of each reality covers up the truth there's nothing at all, just the rapidity of the arising and falling of realities, changing all the time. So life goes along by conditions quite unknown until there is understanding of what it is.

It's so useless to cling because there is no one at all and the object of clinging has already fallen away.

Zoom jottings 23

Letting go of Desire for Understanding

There was a question about attaining vipassanā (clear insight) in the Vietnamese discussion. It was stressed that there must be the understanding of reality now. The understanding has to develop on and on.

Is there enough intellectual understanding to become just a little detached from that which hears now? If there is not enough intellectual understanding it cannot condition satipaṭṭhāna, the direct understanding and awareness which has to arise by conditions. Now it is "I" who thinks about hearing and about attaining vipassanā. This is because there's not enough understanding that in truth now there's just a moment of experiencing sound and then it's gone.

It takes time to understand that it's always a dhamma, a reality, which experiences an object, no matter what.

Instead of thinking about vipassanā, what about understanding more and more about what appears now? This is the way to become detached from wanting to understand. Know that everything in life is right now, non-stop. Nothing can be taken for "I" or something permanent at all.

There has to be the letting go of the wanting or desire to understand what appears. Hearing, considering and understanding develop little by little. If it's not this way it's sīlabbataparāmāsa, wrong practice.

> "Suppose, bhikkhus there was a hen with eight, ten, or twelve eggs that she had not covered, incubated, and nurtured properly. Even though such a wish as this might arise in her: 'Oh, that my chicks might pierce their shells with the points of their claws and beaks and hatch safely!' yet the chicks are incapable of piercing their shells with the points of their claws and beaks and hatching safely. For what reason? Because that hen with eight, ten, or twelve eggs had not covered, incubated, and nurtured them properly.
>
> So too, bhikkhus, when a bhikkhu does not dwell devoted to development, even though such a wish as this might arise in him: 'Oh, that my mind might be liberated from the taints by non-clinging!' yet his mind is not liberated from the taints by non-clinging. For what reason? It should be said: because of non-development what? Because of not developing... the Noble Eightfold Path."
>
> *Saṃyutta Nikāya 22:101 The Ship (Translated by Bhikkhu Bodhi)*

Zoom jottings 24

Sammā Saṇkappa (Right Thinking)

There was a question from Duong Tuan in a Vietnamese discussion about sammā saṇkappa, right thinking.

We are discussing vitakka cetasika. At moments of seeing and hearing, no vitakka arises. After these cittas, vitakka is like the "foot of the world" and is needed to experience the object. It "touches" or leads to the object. In the sense door processes the following cittas experience the same object as seeing or hearing because of vitakka leading them to experience that visible object or sound.

When it's right vitakka, sammā saṇkappa, it arises with the citta with paññā, right understanding. If vitakka doesn't touch the object and sati isn't aware of it, paññā cannot arise. Sammā saṇkappa (right thinking) and sammā diṭṭhi (right understanding) make up the understanding part of the 8-fold path. Right vitakka therefore develops to be sammā saṇkappa

All realities are anattā. Learning to consider the truth and hear the truth is right thinking.

We live in the world of nimitta (signs on account of different realities arising and falling away in such rapid succession). All the nimitta are taken for some thing or some one. However, the words of right thinking are that all dhammas are anattā, arising and falling away just for an instant. They are so brief and fleeting like bubbles. We read again and again about the transience and corelessness of dhammas.

> "When the several truths, aspects of dependent origination, methods, and characteristics have become evident to him thus, then formations appear to him as perpetually renewed: 'So these states, it seems, having previously unarisen, arise, and being arisen, they cease'. And they are not only perpetually renewed, but they are also short-lived like dew-drops at sunrise (A.iv,137), like a bubble on water (A. iv,137), like a line drawn on water (A.iv,137)), like a mustard seed on an awl's point (Nd.143), like a lightning flash. (Nd.143)"

Visuddhimagga XX 104 (Translated by Bhikkhu Ñānamoli)

3

October 2020

Zoom jottings 25

The World of Nimitta (Signs)

Nina asked a question about nimitta in an English discussion.

Ajahn asked her what is seen now. Is it visible object or people now? What is seen conditions different shapes and forms so that what appears is something with many details. That is nimitta.

One reality cannot appear, so from birth to death it's the world of nimitta which appears. Reality is not known at all before the Buddha's enlightenment. Each reality appears as nimitta because of the rapidity of the arising and falling away of each one.

What is experienced now is nothing, but there is always the idea of something. Everything is nothing. Everything is nimitta. It's only the image of that which has been conditioned. There is the wrong idea of something permanent and there is clinging to nimitta but it's only the nimitta, no one, no thing. What is left from the flux of rūpa, saññā and other realities are just nimittas but each reality has completely gone. There is no one. We refer to the nimitta anubyañjana (signs and details) as trees, branches and so on but they are not the actual realities which have arisen and fallen away.

> "And what, bhikkhus, is the Dhamma exposition on the theme of burning? It would be better, bhikkhus, for the eye faculty to be lacerated by a red-hot iron pin burning, blazing, and glowing, than for one to grasp the sign (nimitta) through the features (anubyañjana) in a form cognizable by the eye."
>
> Commentary note: "One grasps the sign through the features' (anubyajanaso nimittaggāho) thinking: 'The hands are beautiful, so too the feet, etc.' "
>
> *Saṃyutta Nikāya 35:235 The Exposition on Burning (Translated by Bhikkhu Bodhi)*

Zoom jottings 26

Burning

Lukas raised some questions about awareness in an English discussion. Ajahn Sujin reminded him not to mind about the awareness but to understand what appears now. "Don't try to detect whether it's that which understands or not. Life is just in a moment of experiencing." She also reminded him to be firm about dhammas as anattā. "Just live naturally, as usual, otherwise lobha is there unknown."

Lukas said he day-dreams all the time.

Ajahn Sujin asked about understanding.

L: Only a bit, not all the time.

AS: Is there understanding of the word or the reality now?

L: It's easy to think about the word. There needs to be sati (awareness) to help understand, otherwise it's only intellectual.

AS: So you understand the word "awareness" but you have doubt whether there is awareness.

L: My point is that I don't have any motivation.

AS: Are you interested in knowing what awareness is or whether there is awareness?

L: I'm worried that if there is not awareness there will be a bad rebirth.

AS: What about seeing now? Should everything be the object of understanding? There is no choice, no selection. There is reality no matter what. If there is no understanding, there is no awareness of a reality, one at a time. What is known now? Or do you just want to know awareness, to have awareness?

L: I know what you mean.

AS: No I, there is only a moment of experiencing. Sabbe dhammā anattā. (All realitiies are not self). There is no one, no self, no me. Without awareness there is no understanding. We should not crave or want to have understanding because it's not self, not me, not under my control. There are just different realities appearing by different conditions. This (understanding) will lead to more understanding and confidence of realities as anattā, no wishing or hoping to know this or that because there is no one at all, just different realities. Right awareness of the eightfold path is not just understanding words that condition understanding. That's the wrong idea.

What is real now? There is a new one and another new one and it appears just once in saṃsāra. No one can do anything at all. The seeing now - who makes it arise? The (idea of) self just wants to understand this or that but the only way is to become detached, little by little, detached from taking everything for a permanent reality. It's much shorter (than one imagines) but because of nimitta it appears as something.

> "Bhikkhus, all is burning. And what, bhikkhus, is the all that is burning? The eye is burning, forms are burning, eye-consciousness is burning, eye-contact is burning, and whatever feeling arises with eye-contact as condition—whether pleasant or painful or neither-painful-nor-pleasant—that too is burning. Burning with what? Burning with the fire of lust, with the fire of hatred, with the fire of delusion; burning with birth, ageing, and death; with sorrow, lamentation, pain, displeasure, and despair, I say.
>
> The ear is burning. . . The mind is burning. . . and whatever feeling arises with mind-contact as condition—whether pleasant or painful or neither-painful-nor-pleasant—that too is burning. Burning with what? Burning with the fire of lust, with the fire of hatred, with the fire of delusion; burning with birth, ageing, and death; with sorrow, lamentation, pain, displeasure, and despair, I say."

Saṃyutta Nikāya 35:28 (6) Burning (Translated by Bhikkhu Bodhi)

Zoom jottings 27

The Dear Self

Lukas mentioned he lacked the motivation to practice and had no goal. Ajahn Sujin responded by saying this was the idea of self. Usually there is pre-occupation, the obsession with the self most of the day.

> "Having explored all quarters with the mind, one would simply not attain that dearer than the self in any place; thus is the self dear separately to others - therefore one desiring self should not harm another."
>
> *Udāna 5:1 "Dear" (Translated by Peter Masefield)*

The proof of the Teachings is the understanding of whatever appears now.

There was some discussion about the meaning of paṭipatti. It refers to the reaching (patti) of the particular (paṭi) object (with understanding), paṭipatti. It is not the following of a practice or method.

It's easy to say that everything is anattā but what about "there's no I", "all dhammas are not me" in your own language? Not "me", not anything at all. Understanding leads closer and closer to what appears, to the truth now. Whatever arises and falls away in the world is just a reality.

Life is just in a moment, from moment to moment. It's not me! When it seems to be more than a moment, it's me! There are conditions for dhammas to go on and on. This is understanding dhamma. Without dhammas, there's no world at all. What is taken for the sun or moon or anything are dhammas which arise and fall away all the time.

Zoom jottings 28

Considering the True Words

An Le asked a question in an English discussion about the development of understanding and the danger of ignorance.

At a moment of understanding there is no moha (ignorance), but when there is no understanding, moha is there. When there is understanding it is true and sincere.

All dhammas are anattā (not self). What about sincerity? It all depends on understanding from considering the true words, from hearing more and more so that understanding will be firmer and more confident in the truth.

> "At Savatthı. Bhikkhus, before my enlightenment, while I was still a bodhisatta, not yet fully enlightened, it occurred to me: 'What is the gratification, what is the danger, what is the escape in the case of form? What is the gratification, what is the danger, what is the escape in the case of feeling... perception... volitional formations... consciousness?'
>
> Then, bhikkhus, it occurred to me: 'The pleasure and joy that arise in dependence on form: this is the gratification in form. That form is impermanent, suffering, and subject to change: this is the danger in form. The removal and abandonment of desire and lust for form: this is the escape from form.'
>
> 'The pleasure and joy that arise in dependence on feeling... in dependence on perception... in dependence on volitional formations ... in dependence on consciousness: this is the gratification in consciousness. That consciousness is impermanent, suffering, and subject to change: this is the danger in con-

sciousness. The removal and abandonment of desire and lust for consciousness: this is the escape from consciousness.' "

Saṃyutta Nikāya 26:5 Gratification (Translated by Bhikkhu Bodhi)

Zoom jottings 29

The Proof of Understanding

In a Vietnamese discussion, Nga Hoa raised the topic of sīla for monks and purifying the mind as taught in the Visuddhimagga. She mentioned that wearing brown robes was a reminder about being a monk, so that the mind would not wander as usual. The topic of sīlabbataparāmāsa (clinging to rituals with wrong view) was also raised.

Ajahn Sujin asked everyone if there can there be understanding of what a monk is if there is no understanding of the truth. She said not to mind about what is in the Visuddhimagga or Tipiṭaka because the truth is all about now. There must be patience to understand the truth at this moment.

What is appearing now is not known so there cannot be understanding of what a Bhikkhu is or what is sīlabbataparāmāsa. No one knows the truth so the idea or what is read is wrongly taken for something like sīlabbataparāmāsa, (wrong practice and rituals) instead of understanding the words of the Buddha about now!

If this moment is known as it is, is seeing a monk? Is sīlabbataparāmāsa a monk? If there's no understanding of what appears it's useless to talk about other things because they don't bring any understanding about the present reality appearing now.

The point is not just reading about different dhammas but understanding what appears now as not self, not anything. If there is doubt about sīlabbataparāmāsa it means there's no understanding of this moment.

It was also stressed that the proof of understanding is whether there is such understanding of reality now and whether it's understood that no one one can make such realities arise. Otherwise we're just talking about that which appears without understanding at all.

> "A peaceful bhikkhu: peaceful through the stilling of lust, the stilling of hatred, the stilling of delusion, the stilling of anger, hostility, denigration, insolence, envy, miserliness, hypocrisy, deceitfulness, obstinacy, vehemence, conceit, arrogance, vanity, and heedlessness; of all defilements, all misconduct, all disturbances, all fevers, all afflictions, all unwholesome volitional activities."
>
> *Suttanipāta 4:3 Niddesa I 50, Commentary to The Octad on the Hostile, (Translated by Bhikkhu Bodhi)*

Zoom jottings 30

Wrong Practice and Rituals

In the Vietnamese discussion we considered more about understanding at this moment. This followed the earlier questions about sīlabbataparāmāsa (wrong practice). Nga Hoa asked about understanding whilst reading books, going to the beach or swimming.

Ajahn Sujin asked her whether there can be understanding of what appears now as it is. When there's understanding, there's no sīlabbataparāmāsa.

It's important to just listen to the truth about life now and consider carefully whether it's true or not. When there's no understanding, who can understand the truth? When it's not this way, it's all sīlabbataparāmāsa. One tries and it's the story of "I" at such times.

If there's no avijjā (Ignorance), there's no akusala (unwholesomeness), no misunderstanding about what appears now, no idea of a thing at all. The right understanding is the opposite of attānudiṭṭhi (the wrong understanding of self and things). It's the wrong understanding which leads to sīlabbataparāmāsa. No matter how many different wrong views there are, they all come from sakkāya diṭṭhi (self view) and attānudiṭṭhi as base.

> "As to the various views that arise in the world, householder, 'The world is eternal' or 'The world is not eternal'; or 'The world is finite' or 'The world is infinite'; or 'The soul and the body are the same' or 'The soul is one thing, the body is another'; or 'The Tathāgata exists after death,' or 'The Tathāgata does not exist after death,' or 'The Tathāgata both exists and does not exist after death,' or 'The Tathāgata neither exists nor does not exist after death' these as well as the sixty-two speculative views mentioned in the Brahmajāla: when there is identity view (sakkāya diṭṭhi) these views come to be; when there is no identity view, these views do not come to be."
>
> "But, venerable sir, how does identity view come to be?" "Here, householder, the uninstructed worldling, who has no regard for the noble ones and is unskilled and undisciplined in their Dhamma, who has no regard for the good persons and is unskilled and undisciplined in their Dhamma, regards form as self, or self as possessing form, or form as in self, or self as

> in form. He regards feeling as self... perception as self... volitional formations as self... consciousness as self, or self as possessing consciousness, or consciousness as in self, or self as in consciousness. It is in such a way that identity view comes to be."
>
> *Saṃyutta Nikāya 41:3 Isidatta (2) (Translated by Bhikkhu Bodhi)*

Long asked a question about the computer screen we are looking at. We discussed more about the āsavas, the taints or very subtle kinds of attachment, ignorance and wrong view which "ooze out" even in the sense door processes. Usually there's always "I" or something there all the time, even before what is seen is known as a computer or table.

Zoom jottings 31

Study the Truth Respectfully

Sakkaccabhāvanā means to study the truth respectfully. Such respect for the truth develops in a moment when there is more understanding, little by little. This topic was discussed in the Vietnamese session. As long as there are no conditions for understanding there has to be truthfulness that there is none at all. It means there are no conditions for sati (awareness) of anattā (non-self) now.

Gradually there will be more and more confidence in realities as being anattā. The development of understanding is the only way to gradually eliminate the idea of self. Otherwise there is sīlabbataparāmāsa (wrong practice). Right understanding understands the difference between the right and the wrong paths, otherwise it's not the right path. It's very subtle and takes a long time to eradicate the idea of self and things. The understanding has to be keener and keener, sharper and sharper. When there is no sammā diṭṭhi (right understanding) we live in darkness.

There is no rule about place or time but there can be understanding of seeing now, that reality which just experiences.

We can read about sakkaccabhāvanā in the commentary in the Cariyapiṭaka. These four kinds of bhāvanā referred to:

1. Sabbasambhāra-bhāvanā : developing all kinds of kusala
2. Nirantara-bhāvanā : continuous developing of kusala
3. Cīrakāla-bhāvanā : endless developing of kusala
4. Sakkacca-bhāvanā : developing with respect of kusala

In the Commentary to the Cariyapiṭaka, it mentions how 1) sabbasambhāra-bhāvanā is the complete development of all the Perfections, (2) nirantara-bhāvanā is the development of the Perfections throughout countless asankhyeyya (epochs or great aeons) and aeons without a break of even a single existence, (3) cīrakāla-bhāvanā is the endless development of the Perfections for a long duration of asankheyya and aeons; and (iv) sakkacca-bhāvanā is development of Perfections with respectfulness and truthfulness.

Zoom jottings 32

Soul

Da-Zhuang asked what the difference is between "citta" and "soul".

Ajahn Sujin: The best thing is to understand what is now. Begin to understand what is clear now. Is there anything now?

DZ: Many things like seeing, visible object, hearing and sound.

AS: All around, but no understanding, is that right? For example, seeing now, but no understanding of seeing which sees now. Can the tree see? Can the table see? Seeing is that which experiences and knows the object seen only. The object appears because of seeing. Is seeing real? Does it arise? If it doesn't arise, can there be that which is seen?

There are two different realities, one which arises to experience an object and one which doesn't experience anything. There is seeing and hearing all through life from birth to death. If there were no seeing or hearing could we say there is "I" now? What we call life are just different kinds of experience from moment to moment. If there was no experiencing, there would be no life at all now. Life is whatever appears at each moment. Each one is conditioned, not arising at anyone's will.

Only at the moment of seeing is there seeing. Only at the moment of hearing is there hearing and sound experienced, never to return, only arising once in saṃsāra (the cycle of birth and death). So life is that which can experience and that which cannot experience. In life there are different moments of experience until the end of life, but that's not the end of realities arising.

Citta is that which experiences whatever appears. In the absolute truth, there is no one at all, just conditioned realities arising from moment to moment, life to life. What is left is only shape and form, taken for a permanent thing because of the rapidity of the arising and falling away. What are taken for people and things are just different realities arising and falling away.

"Theravadin - Is the concept of soul (puggala)

derived from the corporeal qualities (rūpas)?

Puggalavadin - Yes.

T: But has a soul also any or all of these qualities?

P: Nay, that cannot truly be said....

T: Or is the concept of soul derived from feeling, from perception, from mental coefficients, from consciousness?

P: Yes (to each aggregate in succession).

T: Is any mental aggregate impermanent, conditioned? Does it happen through a cause? Is it liable to perish, to pass away, to become passionless, to cease, to change?

P: Yes.

T: But has soul also any of these qualities?

P: Nay, that cannot truly be said..."

Kathāvatthu (Points of Controversy) 1, 111 "Derivatives" (Translated by Schwe Zau Aung & Mrs Rhys Davids)

Zoom jottings 33

What is Now?

Ajahn Sujin asked Da-Zhuang where he was and he replied that there is no one, so no one to be anywhere.

Ajahn Sujin: Yes, but in ordinary language where are you? Without paramattha dhammas (absolute realities) can there be concepts?

DZ: No

AS: We answer "I'm in Bangkok or I'm in Taipei" but how much understanding is there when we speak?

DZ: We try to keep awareness in conventional...

AS: Can we do?

DZ: No 'I'. By listening...

AS: So no one at all can do. For example, seeing now. How can there be the highly developed understanding to understand the arising and falling away, to understand nothing at all which arises and falls? What is in the book is all about cittas and cetasikas and functions but has the understanding of one reality at a time come yet?

It's easy to say "concept", like "tree is concept" but who knows seeing just sees now? Otherwise it's only thinking. One has to be truthful to what is seen now because now it's the memory of nimitta, a concept of reality, the idea of something there.

DZ: For liberation, do we all go through understanding the arising and falling of realities? It seems supernatural.

AS: But what is now? Can there be understanding now? It's not supernatural but very natural, only a reality. This is the truth. One reality which experiences now, conditioned just to see, nothing else. It arises just to experience. No one can do anything, no one can stop it. So study dhamma from whatever appears. This is the best thing. No matter whether we talk about seeing, if there's no understanding now of seeing now, it's useless.

> Through hankering for the future,
> Through sorrowing over the past,
> Fools dry up and wither away
> Like a green reed cut down.

Saṃyutta Nikāya 1:10 Forest (Translated by Bhikkhu Bodhi)

Zoom jottings 34

The Chief of Experiencing

There was a discussion about the conditions for seeing to arise at this moment.

It was stressed that there must be the eye-sense and there must be that which impinges on it. Kamma conditions the experience of a pleasant or unpleasant object. All these dhammas are conditioned, arising and falling away, always bringing the idea of some thing because there is no understanding. Just one moment of seeing is so short and cannot be directly experienced. If there were no reality, there could not be the idea of "I see" or some thing existing.

Citta is the chief or leader in experiencing. It just experiences what is there as the object only. If we just talk about the definition it is not like understanding what appears now, such as the reality of seeing consciousness which experiences what is visible.

Is seeing a cat's, a bird's, a crocodile's or that of a fish? No, it's only that which arises to see. In the absolute truth it cannot be taken for anything. Seeing is seeing. It is anattā (not self), suññatā (empty, having fallen away).

The world is that which arises and falls away, never to return. It's only the world of fantasy and dreaming, when there are the ideas of things and people. What is true is the reality arising and falling away from moment to moment. The paramattha dhamma is the absolute reality which is not self, not a thing, no matter in what realm it arises.

> "Suppose, bhikkhus, that a magician or a magician's apprentice would display a magical illusion at a crossroads. A man with good sight would inspect it, ponder it, and carefully investigate it, and it would ap-

pear to him to be void, hollow, insubstantial. For what substance could there be in a magical illusion? So too, bhikkhus, whatever kind of consciousness there is, whether past, future, or present, internal or external, gross or subtle, inferior or superior, far or near: a bhikkhu inspects it, ponders it, and carefully investigates it, and it would appear to him to be void, hollow, insubstantial. For what substance could there be in consciousness"

Saṃyutta Nikāya 22:95 A Lump of Foam (Translated by Bhikkhu Bodhi)

Zoom jottings 35

Dhātu (Element)

The Chinese discussion about different realities continued. There were questions about ear-sense and eye-sense. It seems there are eyes and ears there all the time, just like it seems we are sitting or we are listening and thinking. There are just dhammas falling away all the time. What appears now?

It was stressed that it's useless to know a lot from books and many words but not understand anything about what appears now. There should not be any hurry to understand from the books at all, but understanding what appears now is pariyatti (intellectual right understanding). Listening to anything (or reading anything) which doesn't bring understanding at this moment is not the teaching of the Buddha. It's so very subtle. It must be understanding of that which is appearing as not self.

This is the way that gradually there will be the relief from the burden of the idea of "I" from life to life. Gradually as the development of right understanding increases there will be less and less wrong idea of self. There has to be "no I" from the very beginning when there is a little more understanding.

Whatever arises is dhātu, an element which has a characteristic which cannot be changed at all. It bears its own characteristic. There are elements which are nāma dhātu and those which are rūpa dhātu. They cannot be any different. That's why reality or dhātu is the absolute reality. No one can do anything. The chief of experiencing, the chief nāma dhātu is citta. It cannot arise alone. It needs cetasikas such as phassa which contacts the object. The chief cannot do anything, it just experiences the object, like the king. The cetasikas condition the citta to be different, to be wholesome or unwholesome, for example.

> "Just as in saying, 'the king has arrived.' it is clear that he does not come alone without his attendants, but comes attended by his retinue, so this consciousness should be understood to have arisen with more than fifty moral (mental) phenomena. But it may be said that consciousness has arisen in the sense of a forerunner."
>
> *Atthasālinī (The Expositor) 1, Part 11, Ch 1 (Translated by Pe Maung Tin)*

4

November 2020

Zoom jottings 36

The Value of Patience

Ajahn Sujin reminded us that whatever reality arises, it is only once in saṃsāra (the cycle of births and deaths). There is never an "I", just different realities arising and falling away. All gone!

Nina commented that paññā (right understanding) arises so seldom.

Ajahn Sujin: That's the idea of self, always thinking about "I". Nothing can be done, only understanding. If there is no understanding at this moment, how can there be other moments of understanding?

Nina mentioned there's not enough, pariyatti (intellectual right understanding).

AS: The question is "I" again. How long? How from? It's not a matter of thinking. What appears now is conditioned. Before paññā, it's ignorance.

Later it was stressed that if anyone tries not to think about self, it's there. Whatever one does in a day is for oneself. No "I" is quite a relief, letting go of the wrong understanding. suññatā means no thing at all.

There was also mention of cira kāla bhāvanā and sakacca bhāvanā. These refer to how long it takes before there can be understanding of what the Buddha taught and the understanding respectfully of each word as being true.

All dhammas are anattā. Understanding the value of patience brings about all kinds of kusala (wholesome states) and good results. Paññā sees there's no need to doubt, no need to try at all. There are just saṅkhāra dhammas. If this isn't understood one just listens for oneself for "I who knows" or "I who wishes to know". Each word can bring the understanding of "no me", "no self". If there's no understanding and awareness now, whatever appears is gone with ignorance again.

> "Patience (khanti pāramī) is the unimpeded weapon of the good in the development of noble qualities, for it dispels anger, the opposite of all such qualities, without residue. It is the adornment of those capable of vanquishing the foe; the strength of recluses and brahmins; a stream of water extinguishing the fire of anger; the basis for acquiring a good repu-

tation; a mantra for quelling the poisonous speech of evil people; the supreme source of constancy in those established in restraint. Patience is an ocean on account of its depth; a shore bounding the great ocean of hatred; a panel closing off the door to the plane of misery; a staircase ascending to the worlds of gods and Brahmās; the ground for the habitation of all noble qualities; the supreme purification of body, speech, and mind."

Commentary to the Cariyapiṭaka, A Treatise on the Pāramīs (Translated by Bhikkhu Bodhi)

Zoom jottings 37

Anattā & Suññatā

There was a discussion about how each reality is anattā and suññatā. There is nothing permanent, nothing that can be found in saṃsāra. Whatever arose has gone completely. There is no "I", no thing, nowhere. It's a relief when there is the understanding that there's no "I", to be free from lobha and the idea of self existing, even a little. Suññatā refers to the reality which falls away instantly and has completely gone. There can be listening with understanding of whatever truth can be penetrated until it's direct understanding, satipaṭṭhāna and vipassanā ñāṇa (insight).

There was a question about nimitta. Something is seen, that is the nimitta of what is seen. All realities appear by way of nimitta, the sign or mark of reality. There are nimittas of all conditioned realities.

We live in the world of nimitta and fantasies all the time because there is no understanding of the truth of the arising and falling away of realities. It looks like something with shape and form, so we say we see flowers and a table but there must be the absolute reality which only appears by way of nimitta. It's made known by concepts, such as "flowers" and "table". The concepts make known what appears and the reality doesn't appear as it is.

> "Bhikkhus, forms are impermanent. What is impermanent is suffering. What is suffering is non-self. What is non-self should be seen as it really is with correct wisdom thus: 'This is not mine, this I am not, this is not my self.'
>
> Sounds... Odours... Tastes... Tactile objects... Mental phenomena are impermanent. What is impermanent is suffering. What is suffering is non-self. What is non-self should be seen as it really is with correct wisdom thus: 'This is not mine, this I am not, this is not my self."

Saṃyutta Nikāya 35:4 The External as Impermanent (Translated by Bhikkhu Bodhi)

Zoom jottings 38

Where is the World?

There were some questions raised about problems in different situations in daily life. How should they be solved? Ajahn Sujin stressed that trying to solve the problems of the world by ways other than the development of the path taught by the Buddha doesn't work at all. This is because there is no understanding of the truth.

The Buddha referred to three kinds of loka (world). There is the world that is taken for beings (satta loka), the world taken for the universe of stars, sun, moon, geographic world and so on (okāsa loka) and the world of conditioned, absolute realities (saṅkhāra loka).

The world in the absolute sense are the realities which arise and fall in split seconds, continuously, all the time, unknown. So the true meaning of the world is that which arises and falls away.

When we think of the world with people and places this is only thinking about what has been experienced through different sense doors. It seems that the whole world is there with many different people and things but in truth the world lasts just for one moment. The citta arises and experiences an object and then falls away instantly.

> "Life, person, pleasure, pain - just these alone
> Join in one conscious moment that flicks by.
> Ceased aggregates of those dead or alive
> Are all alike, gone never to return.
> No [world is] born if [consciousness is] not
> Produced; when that is present, then it lives;
> When consciousness dissolves, the world is dead:
> The highest sense this concept will allow" (Nd.1,42).
>
> *Visuddhimagga V11, 39 (Translated by Bhikkhu Ñāṇamoli)*

All questions can be answered by understanding what appears now. Where is the world now?

Zoom jottings 39

The Raft

A Vietnamese friend asked about the analogy of the raft used to cross the water. He said this showed that even the right Dhamma has to be let go of. He asked how it should it be understood.

Ajahn Sujin asked what appears now to be understood as it is? If it's not now, what can be understood? Is there anything to be understood? Hearing now, who makes it arise? Can it stay longer? It falls away instantly as not self. This is not just at the moment of death, but all the time. Whatever arises falls away instantly. It's nowhere.

In other words, that which falls away instantly is dukkha, unsatisfactory. It's not worth clinging to at all. This is what the raft simile is referring to.

> "I teach, bhikkhus, even the abandoning of desire and attachment to such peaceful and sublime states as serenity and insight, how much more so to that low, vulgar, contemptible, coarse, and impure thing that this foolish Ariṭṭha sees as harmless when he says that there is no obstruction in desire and lust for the five cords of sensual pleasure."
>
> *Majjhima Nikāya 22 Commentary, The Simile of the Raft (Translated by Bhikkhu Bodhi)*

Phong asked about the twenty kinds of sakkāya diṭṭhi (wrong view of self).

Ajahn asked whether there is the idea of I'm seeing or I'm sitting now. At the moment of taking something for "I", like seeing or hearing, is it true or is it just a reality which arises and falls away? Without understanding, there's always the idea of "I see". The wrong idea takes what appears as "I", "I like", "I am".

Phong asked about the difference between "my hand" and "a person's hand". Ajahn asked if the other's hand was his hand. In reality, it's attānūdiṭṭhi (wrong idea of something or someone) when the other hand is taken for something, What is touched is hardness, but there's the idea of a hand as something permanent. It's the wrong understanding which brings more miccha diṭṭhi.

Right understanding at just that moment is letting go just a very little of such wrong understanding.

Zoom jottings 40

The Magic Show

There was a discussion about the characteristic of hardness which is touched. Hardness is the characteristic of paṭhavī dhātu, one of the four primary rūpas. A friend asked a question about having paññā (right understanding) immediately to understand what is heard about hardness or whether it is just thinking about concepts.

If one tries to think about hardness or tries to be aware or understand it, it's diṭṭhi, wrong understanding. Forget about how much or little paññā there is. What appears now? Is there seeing now of the particular rūpa, visible object? It impinges on eye-sense by conditions for seeing to arise. That's all.

We live in the world of Māyā, the magic show or fantasy like in a movie, from beginning to end. It's the same as life from birth to death.

> "Consciousness is like a magical illusion (māyā) in the sense that it is insubstantial and cannot be grasped. Consciousness is even more transient and fleeting than a magical illusion. For it gives the impression that a person comes and goes, stands and sits, with the same mind, but the mind is different in each of these activities. Consciousness deceives the multitude like a magical illusion."

Saṃyutta Nikāya 22:95 Commentary, A Lump of Foam (Translated by Bhikkhu Bodhi)

Tinh asked about intellectual understanding as we cannot penetrate reality as it is. Ajahn Sujin replied that as long as there is the idea of "I", it's impossible to let go of anything because of the ignorance of the arising and falling away of realities. There is nimitta of reality and then the concept of everything as some thing. If no reality arises, is there a world? Without reality, there's no idea of grass, bird, worm. There is just nothing, something, nothing all the time.

The question "where am I?" really means where is seeing, where is hearing, where is thinking? They are all gone, nowhere at all. We don't need to look for anything. Whatever arises does so by conditions.

Zoom jottings 41

Why Bother?

Friends from Taiwan and China raised questions in a Chinese discussion:

Yuan: If there's no I, then why bother about kusala and akusala (wholesome and unwholesome consciousness)?

Ajahn Sujin: Everything is dhamma. There cannot be "I". Hardness is not anyone. It cannot be changed. Is kusala real? Is akusala real?

Y: Yes, real.

AS: So where is it now? Is it real at that moment? What is real now? Is there you now?

Yuan repeats her question about kusala and akusala and avoiding the latter.

AS: There is thinking about kusala but is there kusala now to be known?

Y: Kusala is mettā (loving kindness).

AS: What is kusala? What is dhamma?

Hui Yueh: That which can be directly experienced.

AS: Why is it real? Consider each word carefully.

Da-Zhuan: It's the object of the six doors.

AS: That's too far. What is real now?

Hui Yueh: Realities arising and falling which can be known.

AS: That's the story of dhamma arising and falling.

Hui Yueh: Sound.

We had further discussion about sounds. Hardness of different kinds and degrees of hardness and softness condition different sounds. They cannot arise without the hardness. There must be the impact, like when you put something on the table, there is the impact which conditions the sound.

The world can be broken into tiny elements. Only one can be known at a time. Each one arises and falls. Like the world of magic, we live in the world of nimitta, the world of mirages. Only one reality appears.

> "Suppose, bhikkhus, that in the last month of the hot season, at high noon, a shimmering mirage appears. A man with good sight would inspect it, ponder it, and carefully investigate it, and it would appear to him to be void, hollow, insubstantial. For what substance could there be in a mirage? So too, bhikkhus, whatever kind of perception there is, whether past, future, or present, internal or external, gross or sub-

> tle, inferior or superior, far or near: a bhikkhu inspects it, ponders it, and carefully investigates it, and it would appear to him to be void, hollow, insubstantial. For what substance could there be in perception?"
>
> *Saṃyutta Nikāya 22:95 A Lump of Foam(Translated by Bhikkhu Bodhi)*

Citta (consciousness) can only be known by it's nimitta. The citta itself arises and falls so rapidly. It seems that many, many things appear but only a rūpa impinges on the eyeball. All dhammas are anattā, nothing is permanent. This is the difference between not knowing anything and paññā which can understand all dhammas are anattā.

Study the truth of one reality at a time.

Zoom jottings 42

The Bhikkhu's Life

In a Vietnamese discussion it was stressed that one should not give money or anything else which is not according to the rules for a bhikkhu (monk). This is because it destroys the Teachings and causes great harm to the bhikkhu if he accepts such offerings. One should just give the requisites which are useful for him to live and study the Teachings.

Accepting money and not living according to the rules in the Vinaya can lead to rebirth in hell for a bhikkhu.

> "I inform you, bhikkhus, I declare to you that for an immoral man of bad character—one of impure and suspect behavior, secretive in his actions, not

an ascetic though claiming to be one, not a celibate though claiming to be one, inwardly rotten, corrupt, depraved—it would be far better if a strong man were to wrap a tough horsehair rope around both his shins and tighten it so that it cuts through his outer skin, inner skin, flesh, sinews, and bone, until it reaches the marrow. For what reason? Because on that account he might undergo death or deadly pain, but for that reason he would not, with the breakup of the body, after death, be reborn in the plane of misery, in a bad destination, in the lower world, in hell. But when that immoral man... accepts the homage of affluent khattiyas, brahmins, or householders, this leads to his harm and suffering for a long time. With the breakup of the body, after death, he is reborn in the plane of misery, in a bad destination, in the lower world, in hell."

Aṅguttara Nikāya 7:72 (8) Fire (Translated by Bhikkhu Bodhi)

Zoom jottings 43

Giving to a Bhikkhu or a Beggar

"Why is there a difference between donating to a bhikkhu and a beggar?"

A Vietnamese friend raised this question. Tiny Tam helped answer Ajahn Sujin's questions on her behalf:

Ajahn Sujin: Who is the bhikkhu?

TT: The one who has gone forth away from the household life.

AS: Why and what for?

TT: To seek a way to eliminate...

AS: How?

TT By understanding the truth.

AS: How?

TT: By understanding what is appearing now.

AS: How to understand that?

TT: From listening and considering.

AS: Can the lay person listen and understand?

TT: Yes.

AS: There are so many meanings of "bhikkhu". One who sees the danger of saṃsāra vatta (the rounds of birth and death), not just understanding now.

TT: The question was about donating to a bhikkhu.

AS: To chant or for what? According to the Vinaya can a bhikkhu receive money?

TT: No.

AS: So why do you give money to a bhikkhu? Is giving money to a bhikkhu a way to show respect to the Buddha?

TT: No.

AS: At the moment of giving money to the bikkhu you destroy his life and bhikkhuhood because the bhikkhu has left house, family and so on to live as the Buddha lived to follow the Teachings, to have less attachment and kilesa (defilements). It is not sacca (truthful) if he cannot live that life. Would you like to ruin the Teachings in the Suttanta and Vinaya for monks and lay people?

People can develop understanding and become enlightened as lay people. Only when becoming an arahat they must leave the lay life. So the monk is just like the sign for the arahat, wearing yellow robes with no more defilements.

When we see someone in trouble, a friend or a beggar, we can help in any way within our means. However, a monk cannot ask for anything from others except for the requisites allowed according to rules in the Vinaya. We should understand the life of the Buddhist monk and give just what is useful for him to live and study the Teachings.

As the Buddha says, it is so very dangerous for an immoral bhikkhu to not follow the rules and at the same time to continue to consume the food and accept the offerings given by supporters. It is worse than having hot coal or copper balls burning one's mouth.

> "I inform you, bhikkhus, I declare to you that for an immoral man of bad character—one of impure and suspect behavior, secretive in his actions, not an ascetic though claiming to be one, not a celibate though claiming to be one, inwardly rotten, corrupt, depraved—it would be far better if a strong man were to force open his mouth with a hot iron spike—burning, blazing, and glowing—and insert a hot copper ball—burning, blazing, and glowing—which burns one's lips, mouth, tongue, throat, and stomach, and comes out from below, taking along his entrails.
>
> For what reason? Because on that account he might undergo death or deadly pain, but for that reason he would not, with the breakup of the body, after death, be reborn in the plane of misery, in a bad destination, in the lower world, in hell. But when that immoral man of bad character—one of impure and suspect behavior, secretive in his actions, not an ascetic though claiming to be one, not a celibate though claiming to be one, inwardly rotten, corrupt,

> depraved—consumes almsfood given out of faith by affluent khattiyas, brahmins, or householders, this leads to his harm and suffering for a long time. With the breakup of the body, after death, he is reborn in the plane of misery, in a bad destination, in the lower world, in hell
>
> *Aṅguttara Nikāya 7:72 (8) Fire (Translated by Bhikkhu Bodhi)*

Zoom jottings 44

Hearing Again and Again

There was a discussion about the importance of hearing again and again about the present dhammas (realities) in order to understand no self. The understanding gradually wears away ignorance. It doesn't mean one should hurry to understand because that's bound to be with more attachment to "me". Instead understanding itself develops to understand the truth little by little. No one can do anything.

There can be learning about the truth at this moment. That which is seen is no one, no thing. Afterwards there is remembering what is seen as some thing, but it's only thinking. It's a relief when there is understanding because it's not "me", seeing is just seeing! The purpose of such understanding is just for dhammas to appear as they are. Otherwise they are not understood life after life.

The truth is the truth. When there is true understanding of the realities of life one will not to be inclined to try other things which lead away from the right path. Lobha (attachment) is always searching for other solutions.

That which is seen cannot be anything yet, no thing, no person. Where are you? Where is that which is seen? All gone. There is nothing which can be kept by anyone. Without phassa (contact), there can be no seeing, no world, no thing at all. What is seen now is just that which appears for such a brief instant.

Nina: It's hard to take it all in.

Ajahn Sujin: You do not see lobha (attachment) yet. It goes everywhere with you. "I cannot" or "I can" is atta (self belief).

The Buddha pointed out that lobha is the teacher and also the student who follows:

> "Bhikkhus, this holy life is lived without students and without a teacher. A bhikkhu who has no students and no teacher dwells happily, in comfort.
>
> And how, bhikkhus, does a bhikkhu who has students and a teacher dwell in suffering, not in comfort? Here, bhikkhus, when a bhikkhu has seen a form with the eye, there arise in him evil unwholesome states, memories and intentions connected with the fetters. They dwell within him. Since those evil unwholesome states dwell within him, he is called 'one who has students.' They assail him. Since evil unwholesome states assail him, he is called 'one who has a teacher.'
>
> Further, when a bhikkhu has heard a sound with the ear... cognized a mental phenomenon with the mind... he is called 'one who has a teacher.'
>
> It is in this way that a bhikkhu who has students and a teacher dwells in suffering, not in comfort."
>
> *Saṃyutta Nikāya 35:151 A Student (Translated by Bhikkhu Bodhi)*

Zoom jottings 45

Preparation for Understanding

Maeve asked a question about the preparation for pariyatti (intellectual) understanding.

Ajahn Sujin stressed that the "I" is still there until paññā (right understanding) arises and understands the anattāness of everything. Whatever dhamma (reality) arises, it's anattā. "Preparation" is clinging to the idea of self, wanting to have more understanding.

All realities which arise and fall away are conditioned. They are saṅkhāra dhammas, conditioned realities. No one can prepare anything.

Saṅkhāra dhammas prepare from moment to moment. It means no one can do anything. There's no need for the idea of "I will try to understand" or "I will prepare to understand" because there is no "me". Pariyatti understanding is the condition for paṭipatti understanding (direct understanding) by beginning to understand the reality appearing now as "no one" and "no thing".

For example, we live in the world of rūpas, the realities which cannot experience anything. Ignorance does not understand them and they are taken for some "thing" which is liked instantly. There is clinging to rūpas, such as what is seen and heard, all day with ideas about people and things existing.

> "How, householder, is one afflicted in body and afflicted in mind? Here, householder, the uninstructed worldling, who is not a seer of the noble ones and is unskilled and undisciplined in their Dhamma, who is not a seer of superior persons and is unskilled and undisciplined in their Dhamma, regards form as self, or self as possessing form, or form as in self, or self

> as in form. He lives obsessed by the notions: 'I am form, form is mine.' As he lives obsessed by these notions, that form of his changes and alters. With the change and alteration of form, there arise in him sorrow, lamentation, pain, displeasure, and despair.
>
> And how, householder, is one afflicted in body but not afflicted in mind? Here, householder, the instructed noble disciple, who is a seer of the noble ones and is skilled and disciplined in their Dhamma, who is a seer of superior persons and is skilled and disciplined in their Dhamma, does not regard form as self, or self as possessing form, or form as in self, or self as in form. He does not live obsessed by the notions: 'I am form, form is mine.' As he lives unobsessed by these notions, that form of his changes and alters. With the change and alteration of form, there do not arise in him sorrow, lamentation, pain, displeasure, and despair..."
>
> *Saṃyutta Nikāya 22:1 Nakulapīta (Translated by Bhikkhu Bodhi)*

Zoom jottings 46

All Gone!

The discussion continued from the question of preparation for understanding and remembering what has been said.

If there is not the understanding of whatever reality appears there cannot be the eradication of self (atta belief) of that reality. It's a relief when there is understanding of what appears, a relief from not understanding anything at all. Lobha (attachment) is the second Noble Truth. There has to be understanding of lobha of no matter what degree as not self. Why think about what's gone and that which hasn't come, wasting time instead of just understanding what is a reality now, not self.

There's no need to try and keep in mind all the words. It depends on conditions what is remembered. All dhammas are anattā, just different realities appearing as nimitta (signs). Whether there is understanding or no understanding, there are just dhammas arising and falling away. Whatever arises does so by conditions. Don't mind about what will be next because there is only this moment. With understanding the idea of "I will" is gone. It's so useless to think about that which has gone.

There was a question about "gone completely" and suññatā. Suññatā means that what arose has gone completely never to arise again. There are always useless thoughts about that which has gone. When we understand by saṅkhāra khandha (referring to the 50 cetasikas), attachment is to sense objects or ideas which have all gone instantly. Whatever arises is so very, very short and it's so very useless to think about that which is no more, worrying and not liking it or clinging to it again and again. "All gone", this is the key. This life will finish and death will come. There will not be this person any more and in truth there is not this person at all now. There is just that which appears now.

> "At Sāvatthī. 'Bhikkhus, form is impermanent, both of the past and the future, not to speak of the present. Seeing thus, bhikkhus, the instructed noble disciple is indifferent towards form of the past; he does not seek delight in form of the future; and he is practising for revulsion towards form of the present, for its fading away and cessation.
>
> Feeling is impermanent... Perception is impermanent... Volitional formations are impermanent... Consciousness is impermanent, both of the past and the

future, not to speak of the present. Seeing thus, bhikkhus, the instructed noble disciple is indifferent towards consciousness of the past; he does not seek delight in consciousness of the future; and he is practising (paṭipanno) for revulsion towards consciousness of the present, for its fading away and cessation.'"

Saṃyutta Nikāya 22:9 Impermanent in the Three Times (Translated by Bhikkhu Bodhi)

Zoom jottings 47

Once in Saṃsāra!

Whatever arises is by conditions. Angulimāla couldn't have known what would arise next or that he would be fully enlightened. There is life and death at this moment. Who knows what will be the next moment. It may be death, the end of this life, the end of this person. What arises after this death is birth again, nothing to be afraid of. Meanwhile the best thing in this life is to understand what is there, what appears now.

Touching, seeing, hearing are all gone. It's the way of paññā (right understanding) to let go of ignorance and clinging to that which is no more. It's such a relief to understand there's no "I", no place, no world as we think of it. The arising and falling away of any reality is just once in saṃsāra, the cycle of births and deaths. As understanding develops and the vipassanā ñāṇas arise, there is the understanding of the danger of whatever reality is conditioned. What has already fallen away is empty, nothing. Nothing is there at all, the whole world is gone. This has to be understood more and more clearly, but it cannot be understood clearly by pariyatti (intellectual understanding) and paṭipatti (direct understanding) before vipassanā ñāṇas are realised.

Someone mentioned that visible object doesn't seem to have fallen away. Ajahn Sujin stressed that in order to eradicate lobha, this has to be known.

> "Friend Koṭṭhita, a virtuous bhikkhu should carefully attend to the five aggregates subject to clinging as impermanent, as suffering, as a disease, as a tumour, as a dart, as misery, as an affliction, as alien, as disintegrating, as empty, as non-self."

In the sutta, Sāriputta continues to explain that the ariyan (enlightened) disciples should continue to attend to and understand exactly the same realities as impermanent and so on. This is even true for the arahant:

> "Friend, Koṭṭhita, a bhikkhu who is an arahant should carefully attend to these five aggregates subject to clinging as impermanent, as suffering, as a disease, as a tumour, as a dart, as misery, as an affliction, as alien, as disintegrating, as empty, as non-self. For the arahant, friend, there is nothing further that has to be done and no repetition of what he has already done. However, when these things are developed and cultivated, they lead to a pleasant dwelling in this very life and to mindfulness and clear comprehension."
>
> *Saṃyutta Nikāya 22:122 Virtuous (Translated by Bhikkhu Bodhi)*

5

December 2020

Zoom jottings 48

Nutriment (Āhāra)

Three kinds of nutriment are nāmas (mental dhammas) and one kind is rūpa (physical dhamma).

With regard to the physical āhāra (the edible nutriment), even when we don't eat it still performs its function conditioning the next rūpas. Without it, the body cannot be maintained. When there is no more internal āhāra nutriment, the body needs to eat again.

Trees and plants don't need āhāra paccaya. Only the body needs physical āhāra for life to continue.

Tam Tanh asked about oxygen and air. Ajahn asked if she'd like to discuss these or the absolute truth now.

The second āhāra paccaya is phassa āhāra (contact nutriment, the cetasika). Without phassa, other nāmas (i.e. the citta and cetasikas) cannot experience anything, It is āhāra (nutriment) for all nāmas conditioned by it. At each moment, each reality is conditioned by many other realities. This is the way to understand each dhamma, each reality, is anattā (no self).

The third āhāra paccaya is cetanā āhāra (intention nutriment or "will to do", the cetasika). Without cetanā arising at each moment, there cannot be other kinds of experiencing by the citta and cetasikas. It coordinates their arising at each moment. It is the "will to do", such as the will to live on and on. Whatever follows is because of this "will to do". No one can get out of saṃsāra vata (the rounds of becoming) until paññā (right understanding) is ready to let go, having understood the uselessness of dhammas just arising and falling away each life such as seeing, hearing, pleasant and unpleasant feelings and thinking.

To understand conditions is to understand no self, no thing at all.

The fourth āhāra paccaya is citta āhāra (consciousness nutriment). Citta is the chief in experiencing. Without citta, there is no experience at all.

The four āhāras are just different conditions, showing there is no one at all. There's no point in just reading the meaning and explanation but there has to be the understanding of the reality that the words represent. There is phassa now, for example, but it cannot be known because even the understanding of nāma, that which experiences is not known yet. Study to understand that which is appearing now! There will be āhāra (nutriment) for cittas and life to go on forever when there is no right understanding developed.

When there is understanding of what is in the book, there's

no need to remember the words because the meaning is not forgotten. There is sacca pāramī, the moment of understanding the truth, letting go of the idea of self little by little. People think that sacca is the Four Noble Truths, but it's now. As understanding develops there is sacca of each stage. Without sacca there cannot be the experience of the Four Noble Truths at all.

> "And what is nutriment, what is the origin of nutriment, what is the cessation of nutriment, what is the way leading to the cessation of nutriment? There are four kinds of nutriment for the maintenance of beings that already have come to be and for the support of those seeking new existence. What four? They are: physical food as nutriment, gross or subtle; contact as the second; mental volition as the third; and consciousness as the fourth. With the arising of craving there is the arising of nutriment. With the cessation of craving there is the cessation of nutriment. The way leading to the cessation of nutriment is just this Noble Eightfold Path; that is, right view, right intention, right speech, right action, right livelihood, right effort, right mindfulness, and right concentration."
>
> *Majjhima Nikāya 9 The Discourse on Right View (Translated by Bhikkhu Ñāṇamoli and Bhikkhu Bodhi)*

6

January 2021

Zoom jottings 49

Sīla (1)

Giao had asked about the five precepts and practising the precepts.

Ajahn Sujin stressed that each word of the Teachings helps to condition understanding of no self. Before hearing the Teachings there is always the idea of oneself from life to life. Each word should be studied carefully.

We keep thinking about sīla (morality) and behaviour, but what about the reality? There should be careful consideration of each word to know that what appears now is not self. For example, we may think about sīla, but it's not known as a dhamma, a reality.

There are so many words and many moments have passed with the idea of self. Dhammas are here and now and then gone. What arises and falls is not known to arise by conditions.

What is sīla now? Sīla is the behaviour of the citta and cetasikas which experience an object. It has to be kusala or akusala (wholesome or unwholesome). Only in the case of the arahat (the fully enlightened being) is the sīla avyakata (neither kusala or akusala).

Ajahn Sujin: What sīla is there now?

Giao: Kusala sīla.

AS: At what moment?

G: At the moment of understanding.

AS: Only. So valuable because without this moment there cannot be more understanding building up by saṅkhāra khandha (the accumulation of all cetasikas other than vedanā and saññā) which is not me, not "I".

Why cannot there be understanding of the exact moment of kusala or akusala?

G: Not understanding

AS: Each reality arises and falls so fast. So intellectual understanding cannot say which is which until satipaṭṭhāna is there. Be truthful to the truth. Is intellectual understanding firm enough yet or not? It needs sacca pāramī. (The perfection of truthfulness).

> "When a man possesses ten qualities, carpenter, I describe him as accomplished in what is wholesome, perfected in what is wholesome, attained to the supreme attainment, an ascetic invincible. [But first of all] I say, it must be understood thus: 'These

are unwholesome habits (akusalā sīlā),' and thus: 'Unwholesome habits originate from this,' and thus: 'Unwholesome habits cease without remainder here.' and thus: 'One practising in this way is practising the way to the cessation of unwholesome habits.' And I say, it must be understood thus: 'These are wholesome habits (kusalā sīlā)', and thus: 'Wholesome habits originate from this,' and thus: 'Wholesome habits cease without remainder here,' and thus: 'One practising in this way is practising the way to the cessation of wholesome habits.' ...

And where do these wholesome habits cease without remainder? Their cessation is stated: here a bhikkhu is virtuous, but he does not identify with his virtue, and he understands as it actually is that deliverance of mind and deliverance by wisdom where these wholesome habits cease without remainder."

Majjhima Nikāya 78 Samaṇamaṇḍikāputta (Translated by Bhikkhu Ñāṇamoli and Bhikkhu Bodhi)

7

February 2021

Zoom jottings 50

Sīla (2)

We discussed more about virati sīla in the Vietnamese discussion.

There are three kinds of abstinences or virati-cetasikas. They are:

Abstinence from wrong speech, vaci-duccarita virati

Abstinence from wrong action, kāya-duccarita virati

Abstinence from wrong livelihood, ājīva-duccarita virati.

All three virati only arise with kusala cittas when there is the opportunity to speak wrongly, to take wrong action such as harming another or for unwholesome speech or action in the course of one's livelihood. Only one can arise at a time in daily life.

When kusala (wholesome) cittas just think about not killing or not speaking harshly, it's not virati, abstaining. When time comes and there is the opportunity, who knows whether kusala or akusala cittas will arise, whether there will be virati or not virati at that time? If kusala cittas with virati arise, one doesn't kill.

If one just abstains from harming the other or speaking harshly without kusala cittas, there is no virati. However when there is abstaining at such a time with kindness it is virati. The abstention at that moment may be with or without understanding.

The important point is that the kusala or akusala cittas are not self. When there's the idea that "I can do" or "I don't do" or "I'm so bad", the idea of self is there which cannot eradicate the wrong idea. Whatever arises is "not me". It's gone, it's not self and it only arises by conditions.

Sīla including virati sīla can only become firm through the development of right understanding of realities as anattā.

Only when wrong view has been eradicated and there is no more idea of a self observing or abstaining from akusala can it be said that there will be no more transgression of the five precepts. There will then be no more killing for example, even when one's life is in danger.

So the higher morality, adhi sīla, is only developed with the right understanding of realities as not self.

> "When that Path has once arisen, not even the thought, 'we will kill a creature', arises in the ariyans."
>
> *Aṭṭhasālinī part 3, Ch 6, Courses of Moral Action (104)*
> *(Translated by Pe Maung Tin)*

Zoom jottings 51

Ānāpānasati

Da-Zhuang asked about ānāpānasati, being aware of breath, during a Chinese discussion.

Ajahn asked him what his purpose was. Does he just want to have ānāpānasati? Is ānāpāna (breath) not just an ordinary dhamma? Is it different from what is hot or cold now? What is now appearing?

In other words, we think of it as something special, but the rūpas referred to as breath are just passing, ordinary dhammas like any other rūpas. What is important is what is appearing now, not looking for something different, like a subtle rūpa.

Ajahn asked him whether it appears now like seeing or hearing? Understanding develops by conditions, not by one's will. The Teachings are for detachment, letting go.

What is the truth of ānāpāna (breath)? If it's real, it must have its own characteristic different from other realities. Is it that which is hard and soft? Usually what we touch is very, very solid but is this rūpa not as solid as what is touched now? It's very deep or subtle to understand because it does not show up like ordinary hardness or softness when it touches body-sense.

Whatever appears as the object of understanding is not self, like now. There is no attention to hardness appearing, no idea of how little is experienced and is gone. The breath is just like that. When there is understanding there is detachment, letting go, no control. When time comes there is the understanding of the reality.

Who knows what will be the object of understanding? All dhammas are anattā. There has to be the letting go of this or that object, no wish for this or that. There can be breath as object unexpectedly but it's just like other earth element (pathavī dhātu) rūpas, no different at all. If anyone tries to understand or wants to have it, lobha (attachment) is there unknown.

When there is understanding of no self, there is no wish to have such and such a reality as object. It depends on conditions what will be the object of understanding. There are always realities, cittas, cetasikas and rūpas. Which one would you like to be aware of? It's you, at such times of wishing, not understanding at all. Paññā (understanding) knows it's the accumulation of attachment and that what appears does so by conditions.

When ānāpāna is experienced, is it different from what is touched now? Without understanding of anattā it's impossible to let go of the idea of self trying. The letting go has to be little by little otherwise lobha (attachment) leads to what one considers to be the desirable object all the time.

Zoom jottings 52

Kusala (wholesome) or Akusala (unwholesome) Cittas now?

There was a discussion about kusala (wholesome) cittas with Yuan in a Chinese discussion. Ajahn Sujin asked her what kusala is and whether there is kusala now?

Yuan replied there was kusala now, pīti, joy for learning.

Ajahn said it was thinking, not understanding. At the moment of seeing, there's no kusala. After seeing, is there kusala? Yuan said she thought there was. Again Ajahn replied that this was thinking, not knowing.

When there's no dāna, sīla or bhāvanā, there must be akusala (unwholesome mental states) unknown. There are many more moments of akusala in a day than kusala.

Khanti pāramī (the perfection of patience) with right understanding has to develop for a long time until there can be understanding of one reality at a time, patiently, truthfully and with confidence in the truth. It's not for "me", just for understanding the absolute truth. When there is awareness of what appears, it doesn't matter what the object is. It's just dhamma that has gone!

Khanti must be developed with paññā to show that there is no one, no thing. The patience is a bodhipakkiya dhamma (factor of enlightenment) which develops at this moment with the understanding of no self. There must also be the wholesome interest (chanda cetasika) in understanding the truth.

> "Patience (khanti pāramī) has the characteristic of acceptance; its function is to endure the desirable and undesirable; its manifestation is tolerance or non-opposition; seeing things as they really are is its proximate cause."
>
> *Commentary to the Cariyapiṭaka, A Treatise on the Pāramīs (Translated by Bhikkhu Bodhi)*

8

March 2021

Zoom jottings 53

Ummagga, the "popping up" of Paññā

I introduced the Ummagga Sutta. Ummagga is paññā at the level of vipassanā ñāṇa which "pops up". It must be paṭivedha (direct realisation) understanding to really "let go" of clinging to the 5 khandhas for understanding to develop. The point is to let go, not to understand the word, but the meaning.

We don't know how many kalāpas of rūpas impinge on the eye-sense, but there must be one which impinges for seeing to arise. Paññā can "pop up" to understand what appears directly.

We discussed how in the rūpa brahma realms, visible object is still seen and sound is still heard but there is no smelling, tasting or experiencing through the body-sense. There is still seeing and hearing is because it's useful to see and hear to understand the Buddha's Teachings. There is no clinging any more in the case of the anāgāmī (having attained the 3rd stage of enlightenment) to sense objects, such as visible object and sound, but there can still be clinging to seeing and hearing. Clinging to bhava (life, existing) can still be to seeing, hearing, thinking and living at a very slight level.

There was also a discussion about the meaning of buddhānussati (wise reflection on the qualities of the Buddha). Only when understanding is developed can there be wise reflection on the Buddha's qualities at anytime without any preparation or special act, but by conditions.

There can be reflection now on the virtues of the one who taught the truth. When there is a moment of understanding, there is the beginning of seeing the truth, getting closer and closer to the Buddha. Likewise, without the understanding of dhammas, there cannot be any dhammānussati, wise reflection on the Dhamma. It's the wise thinking about the truth of reality from considering carefully. Thus it is dhammānussati that leads to satipaṭṭhāna but it's not satipaṭṭhāna itself.

Only an ariyan (enlightened) disciple can attain upacāra samādhi (access concentration)) with buddhānussati, dhammānussati or sanghānussati because of the degree of right understanding required. All wrong views must have been eradicated. In the Ummagga Sutta we read about the importance of understanding:

> "I have taught many teachings, bhikkhu: discourses, mixed prose and verse, expositions, verses, inspired utterances, quotations, birth stories, amazing accounts, and questions-and-answers. If, after learning the mean-

> ing and Dhamma of even a four-line verse, one practices in accordance with the Dhamma, that is enough for one to be called 'a learned expert on the Dhamma.'"

The "learned expert" is the one with "ummagga", understanding of the degree of vipassanā ñāṇa who clearly understands one world, one reality appearing, at a time, that which arises falls away immediately. The understanding "pops up" unexpectedly to realise the truth. This is the opposite of when attachment keeps talking about the story of the Dhamma, not understanding the reality.

After the first vipassanā ñāṇa, there must be ñāta pariññā (understanding of what has been known) which gets used to that which has been clearly known as not self. What has been understood has to be applied to other realities arising in daily life until there is the direct, clear understanding of paccaya (conditions) of what appears without words. This is udayabaya ñāṇa (the stage of insight) when it's clear that what arises is by conditions.

> "Here, bhikkhu, a bhikkhu has heard: 'This is suffering,' and he sees the meaning of this, having pierced through it with wisdom. He has heard: 'This is the origin of suffering,' and he sees the meaning of this, having pierced through it with wisdom. He has heard: 'This is the cessation of suffering,' and he sees the meaning of this, having pierced through it with wisdom. He has heard: 'This is the way leading to the cessation of suffering,' and he sees the meaning of this, having pierced through it with wisdom. It is in this way that one is learned, of penetrative wisdom."
>
> *Aṅguttara Nikāya, 4:186 (6) Ummagga Sutta (Translated by Bhikkhu Bodhi)*

Zoom jottings 54

Bhava (existing) and Bhāva (nature)

Bhava and bhāva are two different terms. Each reality has its bhāva (nature or essence). For example it may have its bhāva to be soft or hard. The bhāva cannot be changed. The bhāva of kamma is cetanā (intention). Sabhāva dhammas refer to those realities with bhāva (a characteristic) which can be known.

Strong clinging conditions bhava (existing or becoming) as we read in paticca samuppāda. Bhava in this context is of two kinds, kamma bhava and upapatti bhava. Kamma bhava conditions upapatti bhava (becoming).

Bhavāsava which has been accumulated is the fine clinging to life or existing. It is common to each life. This kind of clinging arises in the very first mind process in life before there is any sense door experience or story yet. There can be clinging to life with or without wrong view.

The anāgāmī is reborn in the brahma realm because of no more kāmāsava, but still there is bhavāsava. There is still clinging to life and different experiences even thought there is no more clinging to sense objects, For the arahat, all āsavas are completely eradicated so the arahat is referred to as kīnāsava (without āsavas or anusayas, latent tendencies of akusala, of any kind).

> "It was said: 'With clinging as condition there is existence.' How that is so, Ānanda, should be understood in this way: If there were absolutely and utterly no clinging of any kind anywhere - that is no clinging to sense pleasures, clinging to views, clinging to precepts and observances, or clinging to the doctrine of self - then, in the complete absence of clinging, would existence be discerned?'

'Certainly not, venerable sir.'

'Therefore, Ānanda, this is the cause, source, origin, and condition for existence, namely, clinging.' "

Dīgha Nikāya 15 The Great Discourse on Causation (Translated by Bhikkhu Bodhi.)

Zoom jottings 55

Groups of Rūpas

Harji asked me about which rūpas condition each other and I gave these details in brief. I suggested we need to consider the various conditions carefully. (All the details can be found in the Paṭṭhāna, the Book of Abhidhamma.) Here is a little more detail.

1. By aññamaññā paccaya (mutuality condition) the citta and cetasikas arising together mutually condition each other.

This is also true for the 4 great elements, the earth, air, fire and water elements. They mutually condition each other but not the other rūpas.

Also by this condition, just at the moment of birth, the birth consciousness (paṭisandhi citta) and the heart-base (hadāya vatthu) mutually condition each other. At this moment only the heart-base arises at the same moment as the citta which it is a support for. (There are two other groups of rūpas which arise at the same first moment, but they do not condition the citta.)

2. By nissaya paccaya (support condition) again the citta and accompanying cetasikas condition each other by way of being a support.

The 4 great elements also mutually support each other.

By nissaya paccaya cittas and cetasikas support the cittaja rūpas. The cittaja rūpas are the rūpas conditioned by citta.

When they are conditioned by citta they arise at the first moment of citta, so they arise together with the citta and are conditioned by the citta. For example, when speaking, the rūpas are conditioned by citta but they don't mutually condition the citta as a support.

This is also true in the case of the 4 great elements which condition the upādā (derived) rūpas by way of supporting them, but the upādā rūpas do not support the 4 great elements or other upādā rūpas in this way.

Again the paṭisandhi citta and hadāya vatthu condition each other by nissaya paccaya. They are a support for each other.

Finally, the eye-base conditions the eye-consciousness when it arises. The eye base has to have already arisen. The same applies to the other sense bases conditioning hearing, smelling, tasting and body-consciousness.

3. By sahājāta paccaya (conascence condition) again the citta and associated cetasikas arising together condition each other by conascence.

The 4 great elements also condition each other by conascence and so do the paṭisandhi citta and hadāya vatthu.

By this condition the paṭisandhi citta also conditions the other two groups of rūpas arising with it at birth. These are the body-sense group of rūpas and the masculinity/femininity group. These groups of rūpas do not, however, condition the paṭisandhi citta.

Again the citta and cetasikas arising together are sahājāta paccaya for the cittaja rūpas arising at the same moment. They arise at the uppāda khaṇa (arising moment) of citta. A citta has 3 moments, the arising moment (uppāda khaṇa), presence moment (tiṭṭhi khaṇa) and falling moment (bhaṅga khaṇa).

The rūpas are not sahājāta paccaya for the citta and cetasikas.

Finally the 4 great elements condition the upādā (derived) rūpas by this condition but the upādā rūpas do not condition the

4 great elements or each other in this way. It seems the odour conditions the taste in this way, for example, but it's because there are countless experiences of taste and odour with thinking in between which makes it seem like this.

The detail shows the intricacy of the nature of conditionality and how it's impossible for there to be any self that can control or condition the arising of any reality in life.

> "This dependent arising, Ānanda, is deep and it appears deep. Because of not understanding and not penetrating the Dhamma, Ānanda, this generation has become like a tangled skein, like a knotted ball of thread, like matted rushes and reeds, and does not pass beyond saṃsāra with its plane of misery, unfortunate destinations, and lower realms."
>
> *Dīgha Nikāya 15 The Great Discourse on Causation (Translated by Bhikkhu Bodhi)*

9

April 2021

Zoom jottings 56

Sacca Pāramī (the perfection of truthfulness)

In a Chinese discussion, Lily mentioned having unwholesome reactions in various situations. Ajahn Sujin asked her whether there had been any wise consideration about the present moment before hearing the Buddha's Teachings.

Ajahn Sujin: Do you own anything now? There is wasting time all the time with ignorance when there is no understanding of what appears now. Without the development of the pāramīs (perfections), it's impossible to understand the truth. Understand whatever is there by conditions as not self. When there is firm confidence there is adiṭṭhāna (resolution) pāramī, along with viriya (effort) pāramī and sacca (truthfulness) pāramī.

Is anyone brave enough to let go the idea of self now? Only sacca pāramī. Not yet! It develops by itself naturally with right understanding, understanding the truth of whatever appears now.

> "Whatever tastes there are on earth,
> truth is the sweetest of those tastes;
> firm in truth, ascetics and brahmins
> cross to the beyond of birth and death. *(Ja V 491)*...
>
> Of these tastes, truth is the sweetest, the sweetest or the most excellent, the best, supreme; for such tastes as those of roots nourish the body and bring defiled pleasure; but the taste of truth - truth as abstinence and truthful speech - nourishes the mind with serenity and insight and brings undefiled pleasure; the taste of liberation is sweet because it is permeated by the taste of the supreme truth; and the taste of the meaning and taste of the Dhamma are sweet because they occur in dependence on the meaning and the Dhamma that are the means for achieving that [taste of liberation]."
>
> *Suttanipāta 1:10 Commentary to Ālavaka Sutta (Translated by Bhikkhu Bodhi)*

Zoom jottings 57

Meditation

A friend mentioned she no longer goes to meditation centres.

It depends on right understanding which has been accumulated to let go of the wrong understanding that there needs to be a practice and a particular place to follow the path. Much more subtle understanding has to develop to know what appears now, however. There is no one at all who can be aware or understand anything. There is no "you" or "me", no person in reality. There has to be more and more understanding of "sacca", what is true now. Moments of listening, discussing and wise consideration about the present realities are very precious.

Lukas mentioned meditation as taught in the Visuddhimagga including awareness of the body and bodily feelings. Ajahn Sujin asked him what meditation was and whether there is meditation now. We need to consider the Buddha's words carefully. Whatever can be understood now is better than going somewhere to meditate. She asked if it is "I" that tries to understand and be aware. There can be reading with or without understanding. When it's without understanding, one just remembers the words from different pages.

Lukas mentioned the 40 objects of samatha (calmness). Ajahn asked him if there is no understanding of what appears now, can we talk about samatha?

> "The Blessed One, Brahmin, did not praise every type of meditation, nor did he condemn every type of meditation. What kind of meditation did the Blessed One not praise? Here, Brahmin, someone abides with his mind obsessed by sensual lust, a prey to sensual lust, and he does not understand as it actually is the escape from arisen sensual lust.
>
> While he harbours sensual lust within, he meditates, premeditates, out-meditates, and mis-meditates (jhāyanti pajjhāyanti nijjhāyanti apajjhāyanti). He abides with his mind obsessed by ill will, a prey to ill

> will...with his mind obsessed by sloth and torpor, a prey to sloth and torpor...with his mind obsessed by restlessness and remorse, a prey to restlessness and remorse...with his mind obsessed by doubt within, a prey to doubt, and he does not understand as it actually is the escape from arisen doubt. While he harbours doubt within, he meditates, premeditates, out-meditates, and mis-meditates. The Blessed One did not praise that kind of meditation."
>
> *Majjhima Nikāya 108 With Gopaka Moggalāna (Translated by Bhikkhu Ñānamoli and Bhikkhu Bodhi)*

Zoom jottings 58

Dreaming about how "I can do!"

If there is no understanding now, there cannot be understanding at other moments. There is just dreaming about "How can I do something" all the time, forgetting that there is no "I" from the very beginning. There has to be the right attitude to let go of that wrong understanding which cannot be let go of by ignorance. Paññā performs its function very secretly and gradually! Learn about dhammas to understand what appears now.

When there are conditions no one can stop the appearing of dhamma more and more. From the beginning there has to be the understanding of nāma (the reality which can experience) such as seeing as well as the rūpa (which cannot experience) such as visible object.

Khun Dim mentioned it will take a long time. Ajahn stressed the importance of khanti (patience), viriya (strength or effort) and adiṭṭhāna (determination) which has to be so resolute to let go of the idea of "I will do something". Only paññā assisted by these and the various pāramī (perfections) can do this. When there is understanding that it is "not me", there is no disturbance at that moment.

Vakkali spoke to the Buddha:

> "For a long time, venerable sire, I have wanted to come and see the Blessed one, but I haven't been fit enough to do so."
>
> "Enough, Vakkali! Why do you want to see this foul body? One who sees the Dhamma sees me; one who sees me sees the Dhamma. For in seeing the Dhamma, Vakkali, one sees me; and in seeing me, one sees the Dhamma."
>
> *Saṃyutta Nikāya 22:87 (5) Vakkali (Translated by Bhikkhu Bodhi)*

Zoom jottings 59

Seeing in the Dark

Thang Huong had a question about seeing in a dark room.

Whether seeing in the dark or not, there's only the story of that which is not known as dhamma. There is not understanding the truth of the world, that which is experiencing and that which is experienced. There is just wanting to know what is there. Is there enough understanding of what experiences? If not, there is doubt about what is experienced. If there is just thinking about what is experienced, there is no understanding of the experiencing.

If there is no eye-base, there is no seeing in the light or the dark. No matter what is seen, light or dark, it is only that which is experienced. In the dark, only black colour appears, not other colours, but no matter what, it's just that which appears. That dhamma which experiences sees any colour or the dark. No matter what is said it's different from what is there. Close your eyes and there must be the object which is seen.

There's no "I" to understand what we are talking about. There will be less doubt about the object when there is more understanding of seeing. There is just the object experienced, nothing, no thing in it. There must be more precise understanding of the difference between the experiencing and that which is experienced.

> "Therefore, Bāhiya, you should train yourself that with respect to the seen there will be merely the seen, that with respect to the heard, there will be merely the heard, that with respect to the sensed, there will be merely the sensed, that with respect to the cognised, there will be merely the cognised - so should you, Bāhiya, train yourself."
>
> *Udāna 10 With Bāhiya (Translated by Peter Masefield)*

Zoom jottings 60

Loss of a Dear Sister

Ann's younger sister had suddenly died a few days ago after many difficulties in life.

We discussed a common Thai expression which is used to indicate "kamma is up" or kamma has brought its result.

Death is so very common, like this moment. In ignorance we have the idea that someone has died and it brings great sorrow. Only the understanding of the Dhamma can lead to wise reflection of the truth without the usual unwholesome thoughts.

Whoever dies, no matter when, it's the common condition, just like this moment. Without this understanding there must be a lot of attachment and grief. Actually, there's no one at all now or when death comes.

The point is to let go, little by little. Even when we cry, there are feelings and other realities appearing, but no one, just the sad feeling or other reality conditioned to arise and then gone, just like death at each moment.

We like to sleep and not to experience anything. It's time to rest. Death is just like that. The bhavaṅga (life continuum) cittas follow the new paṭisandhi (birth) citta. There are more experiences in the new life but it's the end of everything in this life. In the new life nothing is known about this life, all the memories of it are gone. It's just like falling asleep.

When you cry, there is thinking about many stories about your sister or this special person but there is not your sister or this person any more. There is a completely new personality who knows nothing about us. It's the way of cittas and cetasikas arising and falling away only. There is no more connection, no more relationship, but there is thinking about my sister, my house, my arm for a moment again and again. There is clinging all the time. That's the way it is.

It's so miraculous to understand reality now as not self! Without understanding it is taken as something or someone from life to life, endlessly. With less ignorance and more understanding it's quite different, less and less akusala (unwholesomeness) such as sadness. The great danger is ignorance, not understanding and attachment, trying and doing with the idea of Self. With paññā (understanding) the feeling is quite different to other moments. These are precious moments in life. It's only paññā which can understand realities as not self and can let go of wrong view and ignorance. When it becomes sharper, the reality appears well. It arises beyond expectation and this is the meaning of anattā. Whatever arises does so unexpectedly and by conditions.

When paññā arises, there is no thought or regret about the past or future.

No regret!

Each life is like this one with no understanding, just ideas of me, my sister or beloved one in ignorance. This is how life keeps going in saṃsāra because of no understanding. Whatever arises is taken for something or someone or for "I" who owns something. We keep thinking of the world as "me", "my sister", "my family" and so on. As long as there is "I", there is "my sister". It's just thinking. She doesn't know you any-more.

Seeing just sees right now but there's always the idea that "I experience". There has to be the understanding that gets closer and closer to the reality which experiences to let go the idea of "I". There is no one. There is no sister, no family member even now. There are just the arising and falling away of cittas, cetasikas and rūpas.

No regret!

> "The young and old, the foolish and the wise, all are stopped short by the power of death, all finally end in death. Of those overcome by death and passing to another world, a father cannot hold back his son, nor relatives a relation. See! While the relatives are looking on and weeping, one by one each mortal is led away like an ox to slaughter.
>
> In this manner the world is afflicted by death and decay. But the wise do not grieve, having realized the nature of the world. You do not know the path by which they came or departed. Not seeing either end you lament in vain. If any benefit is gained by lamenting, the wise would do it. Only a fool would harm himself. Yet through weeping and sorrowing the mind does not become calm, but still more suf-

fering is produced, the body is harmed and one becomes lean and pale, one merely hurts oneself. One cannot protect a departed one (peta) by that means. To grieve is in vain."

Suttanipāta 3:8 The Arrow (Translated by John Ireland)

Zoom jottings 61

Ordaining

Hui Yueh mentioned in a Chinese discussion that we may talk about "not trying" because there is no Self, but "what about becoming a monk or nun?", she asked.

Ajahn Sujin: What for?
HY: The purpose is for ending dukkha or suffering.
AS: Is there dukkha now?
HY: Yes, there is dukkha, so there is the intention to stop it.
AS: Intention cannot stop it. Only paññā (right understanding) can understand it little by little.

Hui Yueh suggested that if one ordains there can be the correcting of the understanding along the way.

AS: If there is no understanding of the Teachings about realities now, what's the use of becoming ordained?

Ajahn Sujin stressed that all the Teachings are about paññā (understanding) and the accumulation of the pāramīs (perfections which develop with paññā) just to understand the truth about what appears now, no matter one is ordained or not. To develop understanding is always the point, not to leave home or do anything without understanding. So before becoming a monk, one should know what it's for. It should be for the eradication of all defilements, to live as an arahat (fully enlightened).

Even if we are not monks, we can follow what monks do in a day by way of good behaviour that is useful and good for everyone. The one who becomes a monk should see the danger of even very slight akusala (unwholesomeness), such as when clinging to food, to what is seen or heard. We can all read the Vinaya. Even slight akusala conditions madness and is dangerous. Lay people can follow as many rules as they like. The way to eradicate kilesa (defilements) is not to become ordained but to understand the truth of different realities.

What is better? To understand what is taught in the Vinaya, Suttas and Abhidhamma as not self or just wanting to be ordained and not understanding the danger of ignorance and other akusala? Just understand one's own accumulations of akusala even now. Is the wanting to become ordained because of attachment rather than the right understanding of what appears now? Without truthfulness we go wrong. Clinging, taṇhā, is the 2nd Noble Truth, the cause of dukkha. There is clinging when there is "wanting to do". There has to be the understanding of the accumulation of one's nature of clinging.

The true monk's life is far away from the attachment of the lay life. If one is untruthful about the real purpose in the beginning when ordaining, it leads to being more and more untruthful. If there is not the understanding of the truth, no matter one is a monk or a lay person, one is not part of the Sangha that one takes refuge in.

Anyone who is a monk should understand the great benefit, otherwise what's the difference? Being a monk means there is paññā which can see the virtues taught by the Buddha and there are the accumulations to eliminate all akusala. It's very different from the lay life. This is why lay people should show respect to monks.

There was a discussion about bad monks. Bad monks are like robbers, as the Buddha said. It's very dangerous to live as a monk without the understanding of the Teachings.

> "*One living as a dissembler is the defiler of the path:* Having taken on the dress of the disciplined, he acts in such a way that people think of him thus: 'he is a forest dweller, one who lives at the foot of a tree, a rag-robe wearer, one who lives by alms round, with few desires, content.' Displaying such dissembling conduct, which appears proper and polished, this person should be understood as 'a defiler of the path' because he defiles the world-transcending path for himself and defiles the path to a good destination for others."
>
> *Suttanipāta, 1:5 Commentary to Cunda Sutta (Translated by Bhikkhu Bodhi)*

The true purpose of the Teachings is for the understanding now that there is no one, no self. There are just conditioned realities from life to life. The monk's life is for the one who can renounce home, family, everything because they are not suitable for him. It is for the one that can live the life of an arahat. The monk cannot enjoy ordinary things like lay-people. Even at the lily-pond, smelling the fragrance is not suitable for a monk. "Bhikkhus" refers to the one who understands.

> "*A bhikkhu:* One is a bhikkhu by having broken seven qualities: the view of the personal entity, doubt, seizing upon good behaviour and observances, lust, hatred, delusion, and conceit."
>
> *Suttanipāta 4:3 Niddesa 1 50, Commentary to The Octad on the Hostile (Translated by Bhikkhu Bodhi)*

Zoom jottings 62

The Worldly Conditions

There was a discussion about patience (khanti). Without understanding, can there be the development of patience no matter whether it's a good or bad situation? It's not me or mine. Whatever fortune, misfortune, happiness or unhappiness there is, it's just there for a moment. The world is just a moment. Patience (or other wholesomeness) is not for anyone, it's just for the moment it arises and then it falls away instantly. When there is understanding, it's the moment of letting go.

Sukin asked a question about the pāramī (perfections).

Ajahn Sujin: What are the pāramīs for?

Sukin: For enlightenment.

AS: It's to understand the truth, sacca, as no one. So there must be right understanding, there must be viriya (courage) for understanding. There must be more and more understanding of no self, otherwise one is enslaved by lobha (attachment) whatever one hears about.

When there is nekkhamma (renunciation) pāramī there is the getting away little by little from attachment to the sense doors as usual. The development of all these pāramīs takes a very long time with more and more understanding required.

When one doesn't think of the result, it's better than thinking "I understand" or "I need to understand more".

The Buddha spoke about the worldly conditions that change all the time: gain and loss, disrepute and fame, blame and praise, pleasure and pain. One minute we're blamed and the next praised, depending on conditions that are beyond control. These worldly conditions are the ups and downs of life. The more understanding and patience, the less susceptible we will be to the worldly conditions

The Buddha exhorts the development of right understanding of whatever appears at the present moment, without selection of any kind and without concern about the result or how much or little understanding there may be.

> "Gain and loss, disrepute and fame,
> blame and praise, pleasure and pain:
> these conditions that people meet
> are impermanent, transient, and subject to change.
>
> A wise and mindful person knows them and sees that they are subject to change. Desirable conditions don't excite his mind nor is he repelled by undesirable conditions.
>
> He has dispelled attraction and repulsion;
> they are gone and no longer present.
> Having known the dustless, sorrowless state,
> he understands rightly and has transcended existence."
>
> *Aṅguttara Nikāya 8:5 (5) World (1) (Translated by Bhikkhu Bodhi)*

Zoom jottings 63

Surgery

It was the day after my foot surgery. Whatever the worldly conditions of happiness, suffering, fame, insignificance, praise, blame, gain or loss, none of it is "me". The world of the reality appearing is just for a moment, no matter through one of the sense doors or through the mind door.

In truth there's no me, no foot, no surgery, just different dhammas (realities) arising and falling away. Whatever arises is anattā, not in anyone's control, arising unexpectedly. The fantasy, the dreams about various situations are all gone instantly with the moments of thinking. Nothing is left at all after the reality has fallen away completely. It's like this from moment to moment.

There should be no expectation of any result when helping others otherwise it's "I" who knows or "I" who wants the others to know. Anattā is covered up all the time.

Share and help those who can see the value of the most precious thing in life, the understanding of each reality, the understanding that each moment is conditioned.

Everyone is going to die and dies each moment now.

> "Insignificant, bhikkhus, is the loss of relatives. The worst thing to lose is wisdom."
>
> "Insignificant, bhikkhus, is the increase of relatives. The best thing in which to increase is wisdom. Therefore, bhikkhus, you should train yourselves thus: 'We will increase in wisdom.' It is in such a way that you should train yourselves."
>
> "Insignificant, bhikkhus, is the loss of wealth. The worst thing to lose is wisdom."
>
> "Insignificant, bhikkhus, is the increase of wealth. The best thing in which to increase is wisdom. Therefore, bhikkhus, you should train yourselves thus: 'We will increase in wisdom.' It is in such a way that you should train yourselves."
>
> "Insignificant, bhikkhus, is the loss of fame. The worst thing to lose is wisdom."
>
> "Insignificant, bhikkhus, is the increase of fame. The best thing in which to increase is wisdom. There-

fore, bhikkhus, you should train yourselves thus: 'We will increase in wisdom.' It is in such a way that you should train yourselves."

Aṅguttara Nikāya 1:76 (6) - 81 (11) (Translated by Bhikkhu Bodhi)

Biography

Sarah Procter Abbott has been studying and sharing the Buddha's teachings as preserved in the Theravāda tradition (in the Pāli language) for over 45 years, under the continuous guidance of the Thai Buddhist teacher Ajahn Sujin Boriharnwanaket. During this time she has helped share the Dhamma in England, Hong Kong, Australia, Vietnam, Taiwan, Thailand, Sri Lanka and other countries. For the past 20 years she and her husband Jonothan have hosted an internet Buddhist discussion group, Dhamma Study Group, which currently has over 1,000 members and an archive of over 170,000 messages. Sarah and Jonothan lived in Hong Kong for 40 years, until moving to Sydney recently. Sarah worked as a psychologist and a teacher.

Further Study

- The Dhamma Study and Support Foundation

  https://www.dhammahome.com/en

- Dhamma Study Group. A discussion forum for anyone interested in understanding the Buddha's teachings.

  https://groups.io/g/dsg/

- Zolag-Books on Buddhism.

  http://www.zolag.co.uk

www.ingramcontent.com/pod-product-compliance
Lightning Source LLC
Chambersburg PA
CBHW051655040426
42446CB00009B/1148
9781897633472